It's All About HIM

How to

Identify and Avoid the

NARCISSIST MALE

Before You Get Hurt

It's All About HIM

How to

Identify and Avoid the

NARCISSIST MALE

Before You Get Hurt

Lisa E. Scott

CFI
Springville, Utah

ISBN 13: 978-1-59955-218-7

Published by CFI, an imprint of Cedar Fort, Inc., 2373 W. 700 S., Springville, UT 84663
Distributed by Cedar Fort, Inc., www.cedarfort.com

LIBRARY OF CONGRESS CATALOGING-IN-PUBLICATION DATA

Scott, Lisa E.
    It's All About Him: How to Identify and Avoid the Narcissist Male Before You Get Hurt / Lisa E. Scott.
        p. cm.
    ISBN 978-1-59955-218-7
    1. Dating (Social customs) 2. Marriage. 3. Narcissism. I. Title.

    HQ801.S4412 2009
    646.7'7019--dc22

                        2008043669

Cover design by Jen Boss
Cover design © 2009 by Lyle Mortimer
Edited and typeset by Heidi Doxey

Printed in the United States of America

10 9 8 7 6 5 4 3 2 1

Printed on acid-free paper

Dedicated

To my family and friends for their unwavering love and support

Contents

Foreword

by Sam Vaknin, PhD

Author of *Malignant Self-Love—Narcissism Revisited*

Awareness of the pernicious epidemy of pathological narcissism has been steadily growing over the last decade and has resulted in a prodigious and copious output of self-help guides, textbooks, and personal memories. Still, in all this cornucopia, it is difficult to find something akin to Lisa's work: part textbook, part self-help tome, part personal and painful memoir.

Narcissists are an elusive breed. They are shape-shifters and the nature of the disorder renders them alien, a sub-species of cunning artificial intelligence. Their ability to mimic human emotions is unsurpassed, their charm sometimes irresistible, and their thespian skills unequalled. Narcissists defy, therefore, well-intentioned compilations of warning signs and batteries of psychological diagnostic tests.

There is scarcely anything more painful than self-delusion. The narcissist is a cardboard cutout, the mere projection of a false self, unable to love, empathize, get intimate, or commit. Loving the narcissist is an exercise in protracted futility that invariably ends in heartbreak. What you see is never what you get. The narcissist is a drug addict. His psychological survival as a coherent, functional whole depends on the attention he garners (often coerces) from others. He is a singleminded, single-purpose automaton. Behind the elaborate facade of these Potemkin humans lurks the void.

The only way to effectively defend against a narcissist is to learn from the harrowing experiences of those who fell prey to the narcissist's advances and were subsequently victimized by him (or, more rarely, her). The emerging genre of victim lit is seriously enhanced by Lisa's contribution. She has gone to great lengths to acquaint herself with the latest scholarly literature and to scrutinize her own encounters with narcissists with brutal honesty.

The result is a compelling narrative: the detailed anatomy of two failed relationships with narcissistic men sagely set in the framework of the most current knowledge about the disorder. It makes for a riveting tour de force through the tortured landscapes of the la-la lands of malignant self-love.

What is a Narcissist?

Selfish men: they need no introduction, do they? We know them all too well. Or do we? At one time, I thought I knew how to spot a selfish man, only to find, years later, I had no clue . . . literally.

When dating, we try to avoid selfish men. We want to date a caring and compassionate man, and any sign of selfishness is a warning sign. Women, pay attention to red flags. They are there for a reason: to warn us. But what happens when there are no red flags?

What if the person you fell in love with never offered up any type of red flag at all? He appeared more caring and sensitive than any man you've ever met. You thought you had finally found your knight in shining armor. You fell madly in love, certain you would spend the rest of your lives together.

Years later, you wake up and realize the man lying in bed next to you is not the man you fell in love with at all. In fact, he's not even close. There is no resemblance between this selfish person and the caring and giving man you fell in love with years ago. You know, the man you thought understood you like no one else? No, that man does not exist. He probably never did.

He put on an act for one purpose: to seduce and control you. And it was for one reason: to ensure you would be present to fulfill his every selfish need for the rest of his life. This is my story, and I know others can relate.

In the beginning, everything was wonderful, right? He treated you like a queen and put you on a pedestal. My ex-husband, Andrew, wrote endless amounts of romantic poetry for me. He treated me so well in the

1

beginning that it seemed too good to be true. I should have listened to the old adage, "If it seems too good to be true, it is" for he was the furthest thing from the truth. I realized in the end that he had been putting on an act to win me over.

Unfortunately, men like Andrew are very good actors, which makes it difficult to see through them. They can emulate emotions better than anyone. While they appear more sympathetic than the average man, the truth is, they are incapable of having strong feelings toward anyone but themselves. They have difficulty feeling love or empathy for anyone. They do not experience these feelings as others do. As a result, doing things for others is pointless to them. Their entire life revolves around doing things to please themselves.

Of course, you're probably thinking to yourself, everyone has feelings. You may think that feelings are instinctual and we are all born with the ability to feel. You're right. All humans have emotions. However, everyone is different in how they relate to their feelings. I am not a mental health professional, but I have learned one basic and fundamental truth about humans and their emotions: some individuals are more in touch with their feelings than others.

Humans have found many ways of numbing themselves in an effort to avoid having to feel. For some, drinking alcohol or doing drugs helps numb unwanted feelings and allows an individual to disconnect from himself for a short while.

In dire circumstances, individuals eventually learn not only how to numb their pain, but develop an ability to disconnect from their feelings altogether. They separate from their emotions because they have learned their feelings do not help them. They only cause them pain.

One of the most well-known theories in psychology is Sigmund Freud's theory that as children, we pass through different psychosexual stages. According to Freud, if a child is over-indulged or under-indulged in any of these stages, it results in what he calls fixation. Fixation describes an adult who is stuck or attached to an earlier childhood mode of satisfaction.

An infant does not see others as indistinguishable from the self. An infant or small child perceives the world as an extension of himself. Children feel that people, particularly mother, are present to cater to their every need. They know that if they cry, they can elicit an immediate response in those around them. They will be presented with food and cradling in response to any fussing or crying on their part. They see others as existing solely for their own purposes.[1]

This type of selfishness is natural for an infant or small child. They must rely on others to meet their needs in order to survive. According to Freud, this extreme selfishness, or narcissism, is a normal psychosexual stage of development between the stages of auto-eroticism and object-libido. In 1914, Freud published an entire article on the subject titled "On Narcissism: An Introduction."[2]

Most children eventually grow out of this narcissistic stage. They grow out of it and learn to understand that others have needs as well. Unfortunately, not everyone grows out of this stage. If they receive too much or too little attention, they may become fixated in this stage, obsessed with getting their needs met at all times. Freud believed fixation can lead to pathological problems later in life, such as personality disorders as an adult.[3]

Narcissism is a character trait that involves self-admiration, self-centeredness, and self-regard. Everyone has some degree of narcissism. It is what motivates us to get dressed and wash our hair in the morning. However, like many things, narcissism falls on a spectrum. To the far right end of this spectrum lies the extreme or pathological narcissist. This person's narcissism is so severe or abnormal that when diagnosed it is classified as Narcissistic Personality Disorder (NPD). Very few people realize that NPD is a real disorder that has been recognized by the American Psychological Association since 1980. In the past, it was often referred to as megalomania. It is an extreme form of narcissism.

This type of pathological narcissism is maladaptive, rigid, and relentless. It is a lifelong pattern of traits and behavior, which signify obsession with oneself to the exclusion of all others. A narcissist lacks empathy and engages in a ruthless pursuit of gratification and dominance.

An individual with NPD has an excessive need for attention and admiration. This need is so intense that it severely damages the person's ability to maintain relationships. This is because they suffer from extreme selfishness and have no regard, whatsoever, for the needs and feelings of others.

This describes the men I have loved—selfish and consumed by their own needs to the point that, eventually, they could no longer see me. It was as if I ceased to exist in their eyes. My story is about these men, or narcissists, in my life, and I tell it so that others who find themselves in a similar situation can recognize it for what it is. Although much of what he does is unconscious, a narcissist is only out for himself. You must understand this. He enters into relationships with women in an effort to fulfill his own unfulfilled needs.

There are many psychological theories on how one develops NPD. There is now recent research that even suggests that personality disorders may have a genetic component.[4]

I want to be clear that in no way am I qualified to offer a professional opinion on how this disorder develops in a person, nor will I attempt to do so. I share my story with you for the following reasons.

First, I have always found it incredibly healing to write. In my opinion, if you don't have a means to channel your pain, it will stay within you and become toxic. Writing this book has been a catharsis for me. Writing and music are outlets I cannot live without.

The second reason I share my story with you is because I have found hearing from others who have had a similar struggle as my own to be very helpful. The majority of literature on the topic of narcissism is written by mental health professionals and clinicians. While these individuals are extremely qualified, they have not experienced what it is like to try to love a narcissist. I do not believe people can truly understand what it is like to love a narcissist unless they have been through it themselves.

In my opinion, individuals who have experienced a similar struggle can connect with one another on a level that far supersedes any other form of therapy. I personally find it very powerful to talk to others who know firsthand what I'm going through. If I am able to connect with one person who relates to my story, and as a result seeks help and support, I will feel good about what I've done. There is help out there, and no one should go through the disillusionment of loving a narcissist alone.

Last but not least, I'm writing this book to build awareness. I believe narcissism is a growing problem in our society, yet not something people recognize or fully understand. My ex-husband joked from day one that he was a narcissist. Unfortunately, I never looked into the true meaning of narcissism until eight years into our relationship when certain events forced me to face the truth about our marriage.

Sadly, today's culture rewards selfish and arrogant behavior. Narcissism is validated and reinforced everywhere you look. We have celebrities who have become famous for being rude, insensitive, and arrogant. We have shock jocks and women like Ann Coulter, who say cruel and mean things about the widows of 9/11 to get attention. American culture rewards this behavior by putting them in the spotlight. The media caters to them.

Today the most photographed and written-about female celebrity is famous for no other reason than her ability to spend her inheritance. Yes, Paris Hilton. She has done nothing to earn this money, and certainly has not made a contribution to the art or welfare of our society. Yet, she is the most popular youth icon of our times.

We consume celebrity gossip and watch entertainment news as if our lives depended on it, as if the lives of these celebrities somehow have an impact on our well-being. We do not know these people, nor is it likely we will ever meet them, but for some reason we are fascinated with what they are wearing and who they are dating.

On February 27, 2007, the Associated Press reported in an article on MSNBC's website, "Today's college students are more narcissistic and self-centered than their predecessors, according to a comprehensive new study by five psychologists who worry that the trend could be harmful to personal relationships and American society."[5]

Throughout my book, I will illustrate how narcissism negatively impacts the quality of our personal relationships. Before I do, I would also like to point out how it impacts us as a society. Look at our economy. Would we be in the mess we're in if CEOs had given any thought to the numerous employee pensions they were stealing from in return for a fat bonus check or a golden parachute? Look at our government. Rod Blagojevich, Governor of Illinois, was caught red-handed trying to sell Obama's Senate seat to the highest bidder, yet he denied it despite all the evidence against him.

I believe our society has been overtaken by pathological narcissism. America has suffered greatly at the hands of individuals who will most certainly go down as some of the most notorious narcissists in history. We can no longer afford to deny the fact that we live in an era of narcissism, where most people are out for themselves and have no regard for how their behavior impacts others.

As historian and moralist Lord Acton said in a letter to Bishop Mandell Creighton in 1887, "Power tends to corrupt, and absolute power corrupts absolutely."

Unrighteous dominion is a term I believe best describes this abuse of power. It can occur in any type of relationship where one person believes he has power over another. In romantic relationships, we often see men adopt this type of behavior. Studies show 75 percent of narcissists are male,[6] which makes sense when you think about the fact that men have more opportunity to practice unrighteous dominion. The majority of people in positions of power are men. Since this memoir is about the narcissistic men in my life, I will refer to narcissists as male throughout my book. However, it is important to note, females can be just as narcissistic as men.

I tell my story to provide insight into the mind of a narcissist. It is important we understand how a narcissist thinks and just what motivates him. I want to help you recognize a narcissist before he takes advantage of you. I will also demonstrate how narcissistic behavior, if continually rewarded and reinforced, will only stall our progress as a society.

Notes

1. Erna Furman, *Helping Young Children Grow* (Madison, CT: International Universities Press, Inc., 1987).
2. Andrew Colman, *Oxford Dictionary of Psychology*, 2nd ed. (New York: Oxford University Press Inc., 2006).
3. Ruth Snowden, *Teach Yourself Freud* (Chicago: Contemporary Books, 2006).
4. Stephen Franzoi, *Psychology, A Journey of Discovery*, (Cincinnati: Atomic Dog Publishing, 2007).
5. MSNBC. "College Students Think They're so Special: Study finds alarming rise in narcissism, self-centeredness in 'Generation Me'" (Associated Press, 2007), accessed Jan 13, 2009: http://www.msnbc.msn.com/id/17349066/.
6. Sam Vaknin, *Malignant Self-Love—Narcissism Revisited*, (Prague: Narcissus Publications, 2006).

Why He Chases You

So you're probably asking yourself why a man so absorbed with himself would have any interest in pursuing a relationship. I've asked myself this many times. What you have to understand is that narcissistic men who seek and chase women are looking for meaning to fill up their emptiness. They want someone to cater to their needs and fill the enormous void they feel inside.

Narcissists need people more than anyone. They have very specific reasons for being in relationships, but they are not built on the universal need we all have, which is to love. Narcissists do not enter or stay in relationships for love. Their motives are quite different. I believe they become involved in relationships in order to ensure their needs are met. It's really that simple . . . nothing more, but certainly nothing less.

I have fallen in love with not just one man who fits this description, but two. I met Andrew when I was twenty-two years old. At twenty-five, we were married. When he was diagnosed with pathological narcissism five years later and we divorced, I swore I would never date another narcissist.

Well, less than two years after my divorce I found myself in another relationship with a full-fledged narcissist. A man I initially thought was the polar opposite of my ex-husband. I was so convinced he was nothing like my ex that when his true colors started to show, I refused to acknowledge them. I looked the other way. I didn't want to accept that I had fallen again for the same type of man.

In both relationships, what I thought was an overly compassionate person was an overly controlling person in disguise. I misread their desire to be with me at all times as passionate love. I later found myself dumbfounded, wondering what happened to the intense love they once had for me. What I came to realize is that neither one of them ever truly loved me. Sure, they told me they loved me. They professed their love for me daily. However, it was an act. They never loved me the way they said they did. They were putting on an act in order to secure and control me. Narcissists can emulate emotions better than anyone. They make great actors.

Narcissists feed off of the attention they get from people. Adoration from others is what fuels them. It is like a drug to them and they are addicted to it. Sam Vaknin, a self-professed narcissist and author of *Malignant Self-Love — Narcissism Revisited* (my bedside companion throughout my divorce, and a book I strongly recommend), calls this drug Narcissistic Supply (NS). NS is any form of attention a narcissist receives from others.[1]

According to Vaknin, there are two types of NS—primary and secondary. Primary NS is the day-to-day changing attention and affirmation a narcissist receives from different people he encounters throughout his day. When he does not receive enough primary NS from strangers or others to fulfill his desires, he turns to what is called secondary NS.

Secondary NS is strictly for backup purposes. Secondary NS is typically obtained from a narcissist's significant other. The significant other is a constant presence in a narcissist's life. Therefore, they are always available and accessible to a narcissist, should he encounter deficient primary NS at some point during the day.

Narcissists need to ensure they have a constant and reliable source of NS at all times. The best way they have found of doing this is to have a significant other in their lives. They do not love this person, nor do they wish to be with this person most of the time. However, it is impossible to control how much attention or primary NS one will receive from the outside world on a daily basis.

Since lack of NS is something a narcissist cannot bear, he must make certain he has a backup form of it that is always available to him. It is for this reason a narcissist seeks to secure a relationship with a woman. He prefers primary NS because it is ever-changing and dynamic, but when unavailable, he will resort to secondary NS . . . from his significant other.

Notes

1. Sam Vaknin, *Malignant Self-Love—Narcissism Revisited*, (Prague: Narcissus Publications, 2006).

Why He Is Fake

The following terms have been used interchangeably in our culture for years: real self, true self, inner child, higher self. These terms refer to the same core part in humans. It is who we are when we feel most authentic or genuine. Our true self is loving, giving, expressive, creative, and spontaneous. Overall, we feel whole and alive when we are in touch with our true self.

In contrast, what has been called the false self, unauthentic self, or public self describes how we feel when we are uncomfortable or strained. Alienated from the true self, our false self is egocentric, selfish, withholding, envious, and critical.

Our true self is who we are when we feel most in touch with ourselves. The false self is often used by individuals as a way to cover up their true feelings. The false self is inhibited and fearful.[1]

Once formed and functioning, the false self stifles the growth of the true self. The more developed one's false self becomes, the more nonexistent the true self becomes. The true self plays no role (active or passive) in the conscious life of a narcissist.

The false self serves many functions to a narcissist, the most important being that it acts as a shield or barrier to anyone who could potentially hurt, upset, or disappoint him. It can absorb any amount of pain. A narcissist typically invents his false self as a child. By inventing it, he develops immunity to any abuse, indifference, smothering, or exploitation he may fall victim to as a child. He does not want to experience the feelings this mistreatment causes. Therefore, he invents a false self to protect himself from the pain.

By projecting a false self to others, a narcissist is able to live in a fantasy world of his own creation. This projection acts as a defense shield to ensure his true self (buried deep within) can never be hurt again. It protects him from the pain of his reality.

The false self also serves to ensure a constant supply of attention or NS is always present. According to Vaknin, when narcissists create and project a false image of who they wish to be, they are either somatic or cerebral. In other words, they either attract attention by applying their bodies or by applying their minds.

A narcissist knows that by perfecting his looks or exhibiting superior intellect or talent, he will obtain the adoration he so badly craves. Once he determines what he possesses that best attracts attention, he will perfect it and hone it like nothing else. Narcissists are addicted to attention and will create and project a false self they are certain will attract the most attention.

The somatic narcissist flaunts his body, exhibits his muscles, and brags about his physical conquests. An example of this type of narcissist would be a professional athlete, model, or stripper.

A cerebral narcissist is an elitist. He uses his intellect, knowledge, or talent to attract attention. An example of a cerebral narcissist would be a politician, writer, or professor.

All narcissists are both cerebral and somatic. However, one type is always dominant in a narcissist. The narcissist may swing between his dominant type and recessive type, but he prefers utilizing one over the other.[2]

A narcissist's life can best be described as an insatiable quest for attention, fame, and glory. He will do whatever it takes to achieve notoriety. You will often find narcissists in professions that cater to their need to be noticed, in a position of authority, or in the spotlight. Below is a list of professions a narcissist may choose in his pursuit to be revered:

Examples of a cerebral narcissist

- politician
- artist
- musician
- professor or teacher
- writer

- actor

Examples of a somatic narcissist

- professional athlete
- fashion model
- stripper
- prostitute
- pornography star
- actor

Please understand I am in no way saying that individuals in these professions are narcissists. Not by any means. I am simply saying that a narcissist may pursue a profession in one of these areas because it furthers his attempts to become well-known and perhaps even famous, which in the end is a narcissist's ultimate fantasy.

Notes

1. Charles Whitfield, *Healing the Child Within* (Deerfield Beach, FL: Health Communications, 1987).
2. Sam Vaknin, *Malignant Self-Love—Narcissism Revisited* (Prague: Narcissus Publications, 2006).

How He Wins You Over

It is during the courting phase of a relationship that a narcissist's false self is most inflated. Everyone puts his best foot forward when initially dating someone. Narcissists go above and beyond this, however, to the point of acting.

In my experience, narcissists have an uncanny ability to figure out what a particular woman wants in a man. They are then able to project this ideal image back to a woman in order to win her over. Narcissists put on a brilliant act when courting a woman. They know exactly how to impress and dazzle you.

You're led to believe this man is your soul mate, and more caring and compassionate than any man you have ever met. You're unaware of the fact that he is putting on an act in order to win your affections. Idealization is at its peak, and the man appears "too good to be true."

It is difficult to avoid falling for a narcissist. They know exactly what you want to hear and exactly who you want them to be. Narcissists are gifted manipulators, who can sweep anyone off their feet. They are charming and irresistible. Above all, they make you feel as though they understand you like no man has or ever will.

To illustrate my point, I have copied a poem below that my ex-husband, Andrew, wrote to me early on in our relationship.

We met, attracted to that from within.
Your look shed depth, understanding, beauty.
You spoke first, giving a fragile boy confidence.

We moved fast, letting ourselves go.
We spoke, hours on end, on our past,
Those times bordering on Madness.

I told you the story, moments of pain, anxiety,
Deep, despairing Melancholy.
Your luminous eyes, radiant smile eased my pain, my existence.
Your wisdom, brilliance, and strength inspired hope.
You taught me how to live—communal compassion.
You educated me on my inner child.
I will nourish that forgotten boy,
Loving him with renewed strength.

Time passed.
Each day, apart or together, we grew closer and stronger.
You broke my shell, allowing me to be a part of the world.
After each failure, we spoke,
Your eyes promised another glorious sunrise together,
Preventing me from falling into
The unsatisfying comforts of Solitude.

The world is my friend,
Its inhabitants my benevolent companions.
Previous hostilities no longer aggravate me.
I stand in crowds and feel one with the world.
I go to places, overcoming bitterness to those around me,
Recognizing their innate goodness.

I let go, I let go.
The monster on my back dwindling,
Dissociating himself from my beleaguered soul.
Last weekend I released the pain, hurt, resentment to some
Higher Power
With no name save Nature.
I am at peace, awakened into passionate love.
I feel; my senses are rejuvenated.
I am Alive.

You are my lover, my friend, my closest ally
In a world with no enemies.

I need you, desire you, crave your touch late at night.
Coming together, seeing your gentle eyes,
Hearing your soothing voice,
I am taken to a place never visited
Love. Liberation. Tranquility
Awaiting your next rapturous glance
Overwhelmed by your warm, simple smile
I love you, Lisa.

Beautiful, isn't it? He is an amazing writer. Sadly, I must tell you the same man who wrote this poem to me in the beginning of our relationship is the same man who said the following to me during our separation: "You know, I'm glad we're getting a divorce. I never did understand why someone would want to have sex with the same person more than once. I mean, been there, done that. What's the point?"

Unfortunately, once a narcissist is victorious and secures the woman he has been chasing, the idealization phase of a relationship passes and reality sets in. He becomes demanding and angry, unaware that the other has needs or a separate self at all. He is not consciously mean. He simply finds it impossible to see others as independent entities, not identical to himself.

He is urgent, preoccupied with himself and with trying to right his chronic imbalance. While many narcissists do not feel the emptiness in their lives, their behavior causes major suffering and angst among those around them.[1] Let's take a look at the narcissists in my life and what I learned from them.

Notes

1   Barbara Engel, *The Jekyll and Hyde Syndrome* (Hoboken, NJ: John Wiley & Sons, Inc., 2007).

My Narcissists

ANDREW

I was only out of college less than a year when I met Andrew. I grew up in the Chicago suburbs. After college graduation, I moved downtown with two of my high school friends. We were living right off Rush Street in the Gold Coast. It was a Tuesday night in the mid-nineties. Michael Jordan was dominating every screen in Chicago, including the one at the Irish pub we liked to frequent.

The place was packed and the Bulls were ahead when I noticed Andrew across the room. He had his back leaning against the wall as he smoked his cigarette like James Dean and peered over at me. Our eyes met and I fell into a trance-like state. I could not take my eyes off of him.

Slowly, he made his way over. He swaggered up to me and just gave me this brooding glance. Not knowing how to respond, I hesitantly said hello and introduced myself. He then told me his name, and we began talking. I had never met someone so unique. He was brilliant. The way he thought fascinated me. He was passionate, articulate, and knowledgeable about everything.

I've always been attracted to intelligent men. What Andrew portrayed, however, was a kind of intelligence I had never seen before—at least not in real life. He told me he was working on his PhD to become a professor and attended graduate school in the city. He explained that as an undergraduate student, he had double majored in history and English. He was now pursuing his PhD in British literature.

Not only was he brilliant, but he was incredibly handsome. He had deep blue eyes, thick, wavy brown hair, full lips, and a chiseled jaw line. He had a great build and was six feet three inches in height. He got a lot of attention for his looks, but at the time I met him, he was more consumed with his intellect than anything else. He became obsessed with his looks much later in our relationship.

The night we met was magical. We could not take our eyes off each other, nor could we stop talking. He told me of poems he had written and would later share with me. He told me he was working on a novel he would someday let me read. I was fascinated and thought I had finally met a true Renaissance man.

We talked for hours into the night. The bar completely emptied out around us, and we didn't even notice. All of a sudden, the bartenders were shouting, "Last call," and we realized the bar was closing. We walked out into the cool spring night. We walked a few blocks until we were standing under an El as a train was moving overhead.

Although I didn't want the night to end, the roaring of the El brought me to my senses, and I began to hail a cab. As the cab approached, Andrew waved it away. He told me he did not want me to leave yet. I must have hailed three cabs, and he turned every one of them away until finally he let me go, after I gave him my phone number.

I went home that night and could not sleep. I sat upright on my couch, staring off into space, lost in thoughts of him. I had never felt such a strong connection to another man in all my life. I felt a pull toward him that was magnetic. No man had ever had this kind of effect on me.

Andrew had learned long ago that he could attract attention (NS) via his intelligence. It worked for him. When a narcissist finds that which will bring him attention, he will master it. It is his livelihood, his lifeblood. For Andrew, this was his intelligence. He was incredibly knowledgeable about every event in history and every piece of literature he could get his hands on. To listen to him talk was intoxicating at times.

After meeting Andrew that fateful night, he picked me up two days later for a date. He took me to Melvin B's, the legendary and now historic outdoor Chicago café and bar, which was always buzzing with beach-goers and roller-bladers in the nineties. Yes, beach-goers. In Chicago, Lake Michigan is our beach and we make the most of it every spring and summer.

After dinner, we walked underneath Lake Shore Drive to Oak Street Beach. We sat in the sand, and he held me in his arms for hours. It was an amazing night as we watched the waves pound the shore and crash against the rocks.

A couple days after our first date, Andrew called me in an urgent state of panic. He needed to talk to me right away. He told me he could not sleep or eat. Something was bothering him terribly. After agreeing to talk to him, he came directly to meet me at the Sears Tower where I worked. We went next door to Yvette's Wintergarden for lunch. Immediately upon sitting down, he proceeded to tell me that he had told a little white lie the night we met.

Now, this should have been a huge red flag. However, the way he explained it made me feel as though I should be flattered. Narcissists have an amazing way of minimizing their lies or faults by using methods of distraction. They are brilliant manipulators.

He explained, "I was so intimidated by your beauty and intrigue the night we met, that I was afraid to tell you my real age. I suspected I might be a year or two younger than you and didn't want to lose out on an opportunity to talk to you. I never thought in my wildest dreams anything would come of our chance encounter. I figured my little white lie would have no impact because you would never give me the time of day again."

As he flattered me, I sat and listened intently. I eventually learned he was a year younger than me, but lied the night we met and said he was a year older. After I told him I understood and it was okay, he proceeded to tell me there was another little thing he wanted to clear up. He explained, "Well, it's about my studies. I do attend school here in the city and I am studying English and history, but I am not quite in graduate school. I'm still completing my undergraduate work, yet fully intend to become a professor some day."

Needless to say, I overlooked it and forgave him. He was convincing and unbelievably charming. I fell madly in love with him and married him less than three years later. I wanted to have his children and grow old with him. Eight years into our relationship and five years into our marriage, we started making plans to have children together. Before that could happen, however, certain events forced me to face the truth about my marriage—the truth that Andrew didn't really love me . . . the truth that he had never loved me.

Upon realizing this, I filed for divorce. After my divorce from Andrew, I was extremely cautious when I dated. I avoided anyone who exhibited even the slightest narcissistic trait. However, less than two years after my divorce from Andrew, I let it happen again. I let the charm of a narcissist pull the wool over my eyes. I fell head over heels for another narcissist.

JAKE

It was a cold February night when I met Jake, less than a year after my divorce from Andrew. I was just getting over a terrible illness where the joints in my legs became so swollen that I lost the ability to walk for weeks. I basically had experienced a severe allergic reaction to penicillin, but it took the doctors more than a month to figure this out. The point I make here is that I was vulnerable. I had been bedridden for almost a month and was just starting to be able to walk again. I believe narcissists prey on you when you're weak because you're more apt to want to believe the lies they tell you. At least I know I was.

I was catching up with some girlfriends at Fulton Lounge in the West Loop. He was strikingly handsome. He had piercing blue eyes that stood out in mad contrast to his dark salt-and-pepper black hair. He had an urban-edgy look about him and stood just under six feet tall, with a solid build and broad shoulders.

Our eyes met. He slowly made his way over to me. Similar to Andrew, he walked right up to me but said nothing. Not knowing how to respond, I extended my hand and introduced myself as if I were at work or something. He told me his name was Jake, and we started talking. He was a bit cynical, but of course I found this intriguing.

I've always been attracted to the mysterious ones. I know this sounds ridiculously cliché, but it's true. Jake was unique. He initially came across as the strong, silent type. This was in stark contrast to Andrew's first impression, so I immediately felt at ease thinking he must be different. His quiet demeanor made me think he was the complete opposite of a narcissist.

Unfortunately, I misread Jake's demeanor for modesty. I later learned he was only quiet in social situations because he spent the entire time making observations about people. He loved to judge people and would comment to me about them later. He always thought others were beneath him. His quiet demeanor was really unapologetic arrogance.

We left the bar to go to a local diner in Greek town. He ordered a vegetarian gyro, which I had never seen before. No meat in the gyro, just french fries, feta and that fabulous tzatziki sauce. This is when I learned he was a vegetarian. We talked about city life and I heard more about what he did for a living. He was an artist, a freelance storyboard artist with amazing talent. This was the first of many wonderful dates.

As soon as the weather turned nice, we started taking long weekend trips together in his Eurovan. Yes, he had an RV and we took it everywhere, whether traveling the countryside or driving down a city street, it didn't matter. We went everywhere in that thing, including several rugby roadtrips across the Midwest. He was a rugby player and loved to travel. He took me places I had never seen before. He was fun, adventurous, and seemed too good to be true.

Unfortunately, I did not proceed with caution as I should have. We eventually moved in together upon his suggestion and within weeks his true colors started to show. His behavior reminded me of Andrew's, yet I refused to see it at first. His sarcasm stopped being so subtle and funny. He became more and more controlling to the point it was manipulative. He criticized me for the littlest things. Everything we did had to be his idea and he was always right. It was all about him, all the time.

Although his behavior was so eerily reminiscent of Andrew's, I refused to acknowledge it. I was not about to admit, after all I had learned, that I had fallen for another narcissist. I lied to myself for months. By the time I ended our relationship, I was depressed and suffered from major anxiety. It was the darkest time of my life and one I hope never to revisit.

Characteristics of a Narcissist

I want to help you recognize a narcissist before he takes advantage of you. I will describe Andrew and Jake's behavior, so you can see how pathological narcissism manifests itself in a relationship.

According to the American Psychological Association, there are nine characteristics of narcissism. The Diagnostic and Statistics Manual (DSM) of mental disorders states Narcissistic Personality Disorder exists when five or more of the nine criteria listed below are met:

1 Feels grandiose and self-important for reasons that are not supported by reality

2 Obsessed with fantasies of unlimited success, fame, power, or omnipotence via his unequalled brilliance (the cerebral narcissist) or bodily beauty and sexual performance (the somatic narcissist)

3 Believes that he is unique and special and can only be understood by and associate with other unique or high-status people

4 Requires excessive admiration, adulation, attention, and affirmation

5 Feels a sense of entitlement

6 Exploits others without guilt or remorse

7 Devoid of empathy

8 Tends to be envious of others or believes that others are envious of him

9 Displays arrogant and haughty behavior

Please allow me to say once again that I am not a mental health professional. You should refer to the Diagnostic and Statistics Manual

(DSM) of Mental Disorders for a professional description of each of the nine criteria. The knowledge I offer is based on my personal experience. Let's take a look at each one of the characteristics.

1. FEELS GRANDIOSE AND SELF-IMPORTANT FOR REASONS THAT ARE NOT SUPPORTED BY REALITY

Narcissists think they are superior to others. They truly believe their opinions and beliefs are more valuable than others'. They think people admire them for their intellect or physical prowess. They support this grandiose image of themselves via their false self. However, their self-inflated view is often not supported by reality, which is why many narcissists are so angry all the time. They refuse to accept the fact that they are not as renowned as they would like to imagine.[1]

Andrew

Andrew made it quite obvious to others that he felt his opinions were superior. He flaunted his intelligence. He spoke to everyone as if he were their teacher, and they had something to learn from him. He considered himself a literary artist and would often compare himself to famous writers, such as Henry Miller or T.S. Eliot. He was condescending in his tone and often sounded as if he was lecturing.

On more than one occasion, after spending time with our friends, he turned to me and said, "Our friends can be so boring sometimes, don't you think? They don't have much to offer, do they?"

Below is an email he once sent me after a night out with his friends:

> I don't really know why I went out. I never have any fun anyway. Brett or Josh will demand I go out. You know, hang out, chill, do that Generation X thing. I say the hell with Generation X, with bars, with the damn bourgeois mentality of the twentieth-century man. Sorry, I don't mean to get worked up like that, but I hate, absolutely hate, going out. So what, so I can meet boring, tedious people. Damn, I am so self-righteous. I go to bars with my friends; I sit there and talk, unless of course with Adam, about nothing of consequence or value. We dispassionately talk about sports, the weather, meaningless subjects—I can't stand it. I no longer want to have conversations of useless value, ones in which I gain nothing but a passing of the time and a lesser opinion of those I consider to be my friends. Let me be! I am so tired . . . ugh . . .

I just want to be left alone. I can no longer deal with the world and its mediocrity. Whatever happened to art, passion, literature, love and beauty."

Like I was saying before I went on one of my many tangents . . . I go to these bars, you know—the young, affluent, just out of college, I work down town 9-5 hangouts. At these joints, everyone (yes, I am stereotyping, but give me the privilege, the beloved honor, the intellectual elitist's God-given hallowed right. Let me generalize, for specifics weigh me down. They are far too tiresome and banal. Let me scour the wretched and decaying world with my wrath of insight) . . . everyone, well, let us say here, most people . . . all looking like clones.

I recall another occasion when Andrew said to me, "You know, I must have been an aristocrat in a former life or my ancestors were aristocrats because I feel like royalty. The life of an aristocrat would have suited me very well, don't you think? Too bad I was born at the wrong time."

Jake

Not all narcissists are so obvious about their arrogance. They certainly will never reveal their true colors until they feel confident they have obtained control of you. Initially, they prefer to appear humble to the outside world. Jake appeared extremely modest the night I met him. However, once a narcissist is alone with those who know him intimately, his arrogance is impossible to deny.

Jake thought his way of thinking was the only way of thinking. He scoffed at anyone who had different beliefs than him. He was a vegetarian and looked down on anyone who ate meat. One time as we were sitting outside at a beautiful café in Playa del Carmen about to order dinner, I told Jake I was thinking of ordering barbecue ribs. He told me not to order ribs because he didn't like me eating meat. After a ridiculous argument, I told him I wasn't changing my mind. In response, he lifted his hand and pointed over at the table immediately next to us where a heavy-set young girl in her early teens was eating a meat dinner with her family.

Loud enough for everyone, including her, to hear he pointed directly at her and said, "You want to eat meat? Go right ahead! You'll be as fat as her then. If that's what you want, then go right ahead . . . be my guest!"

Every narcissist you encounter has a hugely inflated sense of himself. It may take longer to see it in some cases than others, but eventually it will become obvious. Their arrogance will become quite apparent.

2. OBSESSED WITH FANTASIES OF UNLIMITED SUCCESS, FAME, POWER, OR OMNIPOTENCE VIA HIS UNEQUALLED BRILLIANCE (CEREBRAL) OR BODILY BEAUTY AND SEXUAL PERFORMANCE (SOMATIC).

Narcissists are addicted to attention. Securing it is their predominant drive. Fame provides a narcissist with a constant supply of NS. Fame creates a mechanism for which a narcissist can obtain the constant attention he needs. If one is famous, the image he projects of himself is reflected back at him in the eyes of those who revere him. His image is validated as he sees his name in lights or his face on the cover of a magazine. This is the ultimate fantasy for a narcissist.[2]

There is almost nothing a narcissist won't do if he thinks it will bring him fame. To him, there is no such thing as bad publicity. Any publicity is good publicity. An example of this mentality, in its most extreme, is OJ Simpson writing a book about how he would have killed his wife and her lover if he had made it a goal. He needed to let the world know that if he wanted to kill his wife, he could have pulled it off and then proceeded to let everyone know how he would have done it.

An individual has to be extremely desperate for attention to suggest something so horrific and perverse. However, this is exactly the type of behavior you can expect from a narcissist. They are desperately addicted to the limelight. It is like a drug to them, and they will stop at nothing to obtain or, in OJ's case, regain it.

Andrew

Andrew became a high school history teacher. To illustrate how Andrew obtained NS from his students, I've included an email below, which he sent me right after our divorce. He was about to take a month off from teaching. He was looking forward to taking some time off; however, he was a bit concerned at the same time. Why? Because it meant he would no longer have a daily audience of students to hang on his every word. Upon this realization, he sent me the following in an email:

> As I finish off summer school in the next week and begin a month long break, I sense an impending moment of relief juxtaposed with a strong, palatable anxiety.... My sentiment of trepidation naturally occurs from not teaching. For an entire month, I will not get to elaborate on the wonderful debate between Alexander Hamilton and Thomas Jefferson; will not get to passionately tell Tecumseh's Curse (except to the occasional friend or prospective female at a bar); will

not have the opportunity to sell the importance of Andrew Jackson to United States history; will not have the chance to propagate my notion of how Manifest Destiny connects with and relates to the Puritans, the war in Iraq, and our treatment of the Native Americans; will not have the chance to give an extensive, all-consuming, and exhausting lecture on how the Treaty of Versailles shaped the twentieth-century and was ultimately responsible for its failures and horrors; and consequently, I will not be able to proffer an ideology—my ideology—of tolerance, of intellectual curiosity, and of a guarded, reticent hope, a hope not so much in people, but rather in individuals, those who are unique and have big, bold, strong personalities, who move history, rather than being moved by it, those men and women with a vision, a charisma, an ability to shape and craft ideas.

Individuals are wonderful, people are dangerous. Individuals are strong and insatiable, people are weak and full. While individuals stand alone screaming before a crowd, people sit and listen together, mumbling in unison their rejection or adulation depending on what the person next to him thinks. While individuals defy order, people are only too willing to acquiesce.

My best teaching comes from explaining history, its relevance, its complexity, and moreover, in imbibing learning with a liberal, passionate, exuberance. Like Sampson before me, there will be better organized teachers, more creative teachers, more caring teachers, and definitely without question, harder working teachers, but I will say that my class will never be boring or monotonous, because even when discussing the end of the frontier after the Civil War—a topic with seemingly little interest to layman on the street—I will tell an interesting story about how railroad companies and the U.S. government hired ace shooters to ride along on railroad cars and kill buffalo so that one day, the Native Americans, who lost their main means of sustenance, would be forced to either assimilate or move onto reservations, thus, clearing the way for the expansion westward by the dominant white culture.

Jake

Jake's artwork brought him the much-needed attention and admiration he craved, but it was never enough. No matter how much attention a narcissist receives, it is never adequate. Jake was never satisfied with his career as a freelance artist. Although he made a great living and only had to work a few days a month, he was never happy. He wasn't famous or living the dream life he had imagined for himself. A narcissist often has to imagine a different life for himself because the one he has never measures up to his grandiose idea of what it should be.[3]

Jake thought of himself as a world traveler. He loved Jacques Cousteau. At times, I think he thought he was Jacques Cousteau. One time when we were vacationing in the Turks and Caicos, we met a man who was operating boat tours. His name was Bruce. Bruce had just left his family back in Canada to pursue his dream business, which was to charter boats in the Caribbean. He left his wife and two teenage sons at home while he pursued this dream of his. He told us his wife was supportive and didn't mind raising the two teenage boys on her own while he started this new venture.

What was eye-opening to me is that Jake worshipped this man. Jake thought Bruce was the coolest guy in the world for doing this, which made me question whether Jake really wanted to settle down and raise a family together. Of course, in the beginning of our relationship, he told me this is exactly what he wanted. I remember he said, "I realize now why I have always been unsure on whether I would like to have children or not. It's because I've never met a woman that I wanted to be the mother of my children until you."

Remember, this was in the early idealization stage of our relationship. In typical narcissist fashion, he told me exactly what he thought I wanted to hear, but did he mean it? This is what I was starting to question.

Despite my fears, Jake insisted he wanted to settle down with me and have a family together. So we started looking at homes to buy together. It was his idea to do this, not mine. I owned my own place in the city and was quite happy with it. He wanted to buy a home together, so we started looking.

Jake had always rented, despite his good financial standing. He would rather rent than own, he told me, because it was less permanent. The only thing he owned was his beloved RV that he paid cash for years ago. It was easy for him to invest in an RV because it had wheels and could go anywhere. Shortly before I met him, he took a six-month road trip across the country and lived out of his RV. He told me it was his last hurrah as a single man, but I wasn't so sure.

Looking at homes with him was a joke. He pretended he wanted to settle down with me, so we would go out on these ridiculous house-hunting trips with realtors. I don't know if he was trying to convince himself he wanted to settle down or if he was pretending to be interested in looking at these homes simply to amuse me. Whatever the case, it was pointless and exhausting. He found something wrong with every home we looked at, and we looked at countless homes. I had heard every excuse in the book from him on why the particular home we were looking at was not a good buy.

We finally found a home that met all of his extremely high and unrealistic expectations. I couldn't imagine what excuse he would come up with not to buy this home. It was absolutely perfect. When it came time to make an offer, he told me he didn't want to buy it because of the house next door. I was dumbfounded.

The house next door was a million-dollar brick home that had just been built after the tear-down of an older home. It was a beautiful home and could have been featured in any home and design magazine. When I asked Jake what was wrong with the house next door, he told me it threw off the whole neighborhood because it was too modern compared to the rest of the historic homes it sat among.

How a red brick home is too modern I will never understand, but this was his reason for not liking the home. The truth is he found fault with every home we looked at so he would not have to commit. The thought of putting roots down terrifies a narcissist.

I have never seen someone daydream or fantasize about another life more than Jake. The last several months of our relationship, he would lie in bed with my laptop every night and search the Internet for hours. Sometimes I would wake up at 3:00 in the morning and he would still be online looking at property he might buy in other countries. Property in Europe, Costa Rica, Mexico, even Canada . . . anywhere but America. He was cynical about America and would constantly dream and talk about how much better our life would be if we lived in another country.

We started getting into arguments because he said I didn't get enough vacation time for him. He told me he needed to be with someone who could travel the world with him on a moment's notice. Since Jake only had to work a few days a month, he wanted to spend the rest of his time traveling.

I'm a human resources professional and have invested a lot in my career. I have my master's degree and have been published twice in academic journals related to my profession. Despite this, Jake always tried to talk me into taking a job that would give me the summers off or allow me to work from home every day. At one point during our relationship, there was an opportunity for me to pursue a different career at my firm that would allow me to work from home (or remotely) every day of the week. I considered it briefly because of Jake's encouragement to do so, but then quickly realized it was not the type of work I would enjoy. I explained to Jake why I wouldn't enjoy the work, and that I was quite happy in my current career.

Well, Jake was furious with me for not taking this job. He thought if I didn't have to be in the office every day and could work remotely, I could easily work from anywhere. He thought this would then allow us to travel more. I tried to explain that this was not realistic and that I would be unhappy with the type of work the job offered. Since he's incapable of thinking of anyone but himself, it didn't matter what I wanted. He made me feel absolutely horrible for not pursuing that job.

He said, "If you cared about our future, you would take this job. Your job restrains us!"

He even went so far as to tell me that he didn't know if he could be with someone who had to work a nine-to-five job. Let me be clear: Jake was not asking me to give up my career and travel the world with him. I had to work and wanted to work, but he thought he should be able to dictate what kind of job I had.

Another time, he got this idea in his head that he wanted to move to Amsterdam. He wanted us to live on a barge so he could paint all day. He couldn't believe I wasn't interested in doing this. Don't get me wrong— Amsterdam is one of my favorite cities, but he wasn't being realistic or thinking about how we would make a living there. Jake made his living as a freelance artist for advertising agencies. He had to live in a city with a substantial advertising industry like Chicago to maintain his current level of income. Amsterdam, while quaint and beautiful, is not the advertising capital of the world.

Not only was he not being realistic about how we would pay the bills in Amsterdam, but he never gave any thought to what I may have wanted. It didn't matter to him that I enjoyed my career and loved Chicago. No, everything was always about him and what he wanted. He couldn't believe I was not willing to sit and watch him paint for who knows how many years on a barge in Amsterdam.

Living with a narcissist is exhausting. Nothing is ever good enough for him and never will be. He is constantly in a dreamlike state, waiting for his life to begin. While he does this, he drags everyone around him down into his miserable and cynical view of the world.

In my opinion, a narcissist's mood can at times be described as someone with manic-depressive disorder. They're either extremely manic and high on life or horribly negative and cynical. Very rarely will you find them anywhere in the middle. Everything they do is extreme. When they're manic they are unbelievably fun, but when they're not, they are terribly depressing and critical.

3. BELIEVES THAT HE IS UNIQUE AND SPECIAL AND CAN ONLY BE UNDERSTOOD BY AND ASSOCIATE WITH OTHER UNIQUE OR HIGH-STATUS PEOPLE

A narcissist considers himself a rare breed that cannot be understood by just anyone. He feels he is unique and special, while the majority of others are common and ordinary. A narcissist only associates with others of high status or intellect, for he feels only these people can possibly understand him.[4]

Andrew

One evening early on in our relationship, Andrew and I got in an argument because he made a very elitist comment that upset me. I cannot remember exactly what he said, but he basically explained that he was concerned if he pursued an exclusive relationship with me, things could become routine or domestic at some point. Seeing himself as a great literary artist, he did not feel a life of domesticity would suit him well. He explained that he needed stimulation and excitement to reach his artistic potential. Needless to say, I was very upset with him for making this comment and told him I was not sure if I wanted to see him anymore.

The next day, he sent me the following letter:

Dear Lisa,

I know you are busy, and I know I'm the last person in the world you probably want to hear from on one of the busiest days of the month. I am sorry, but I must tell you some things.

First, many of my remarks last night were my thoughts out loud; I was thinking out loud, trying to make sense out of what just happened. I know I can't take back what I said. I am sorry for what I said though for I meant barely any of it. I am not saying this for any reason except that it is the truth. Sometimes my mind, in a manner to contain my random thoughts, works verbally. Unfortunately, you, instead of someone else, bore my thinking out loud. At that moment, I wished I had Adam with which to speak . . . Also, I respect your world and you as a person in that world. My own hostility towards much of that world is a projection, for it is not their fault that I am unable to relate to them. Your world is not frivolous or petty, and I respect that side of you. In fact, I am envious of you for being able to engage in a world I cannot understand. Most of the people I feel this resentment towards are probably nice, interesting individuals.

You do not bore me. You fascinate and intrigue me; every time I see you, you say something funny or intelligent, do some adorable act which proves to me that you are interesting. You have much to offer to me; I am willing to learn from you. You have enabled me to reach my goal in life: Liberation. You gave me faith in a world (female relationships) I had lost complete hope for. I never envisioned myself in a normal, healthy relationship. Throughout my entire life, I can honestly say, I have never, never been in a productive relationship. There was always obsession, then irritation, problems (usually of my own instigating and never resolved) then a breakup. I do not want this with you. I love you.

Last night, you were right. I pulled back into myself, farther into my narcissistic shell. I disengaged the passion, longing, desire I have for you every time I see you. I need you. I was shocked on Monday, while I was away from you about how normal, free, liberated I felt; it felt good. You mean so much to me. I want you to feel that. I have never in my life felt normal, felt able, yes, willing to engage everyday, ordinary people of the world in any manner besides one consisting of superficial discourse. Adam showed me some individuals are not bad. You showed me how most people are essentially good-natured and kind-hearted . . . I am not happy alone, full of anxiety, alienated (mostly through a projection on my own part), in despair. I need companionship. I need you.

My former world—that of being alone—I do like most of the time. But with you, in your company or with your friends, I am happy, content, at peace with myself and with the world. Sometimes though, for instance Saturday night, I must go for a walk, for the inspiration, feelings, intense passionate thought demands that I delve into those realms harder, deeper to find higher meaning. I must learn, for the first time really in my life to manage the world of fancy and passion, the world of the artist, with the world of simple pleasures and companionship, with a world where I can find peace, some semblance of salvation; a world of reality. I believe I have found that world with you; a combination of both of those worlds. Do you remember Saturday night when I mentioned to you that I was utterly enthralled with just being simple, "hanging out?" I do not want to be a recluse lonely artist, no matter how successful I may be. I want companionship. I want love; I have Eros with you.

You do not change me into a boring, mediocre commoner. You give me peace. You need not worry about changing me; the only change I shall make is to lose an inkling of my narcissistic elitism. Do not worry though; I will not, cannot, lose my passion, longing, desire for literature, writing, the arts.

With you in my arms at night and in my thoughts during the day, my writing will be more hopeful, liberating, communal. Without you, my work becomes antagonistic, hostile, full of envy, debauchery, and anxiety. I have no better friend in the world. I share my work with you; my thoughts (all of them sometimes, even the random, dispersed unreflected thoughts, which do not really reflect my true nature and often hurt you) with you; my enflamed, passionate soul with you, for I know that you can understand me. (You are brilliant, with a past which breeds tremendous depth and an understood and appreciated spirituality.)

I love you, realizing this more and more as I write this letter to you. I cannot wait to see you, to see that look in your eyes. I need you; I want you to realize your importance in my life. You are so beautiful, sensuous. I hope I have not hurt you to a point from which we cannot resolve, work out, the confusion, the pain of last night. I just want to make you happy, to make your day better when I see you after your long day at work. Once again, I am sorry for writing on your busiest day; I needed to though. With all my heart, I want to dance in the streets and scream to the world that I am in love and that true love is possible. I want to run joyfully around, yearning for your simple touch. I love you, Lisa.

Narcissists pride themselves on being unique. They wish to be distinct and special. To be compared to others is an absolute insult to them. They think anything common or universally sought is weak and ordinary . . . not to be valued at all.[5]

Whenever I talked to Andrew about having children, he used to say to me, "Breeding is common. Anyone can do it. There's nothing special about it. I don't know what all the fuss is about. I don't understand why you want to have children so badly."

LISA E. SCOTT

Jake

Narcissists believe they are too good to wait in line with the rest of "the herd" as they refer to it. Jake loved to brag about the time, a few years earlier, when he was in Disney World with his adult sister. He put her in a wheelchair so they didn't have to wait in line. She wasn't injured or handicapped in any way, but by putting her in a wheelchair, he was able to push her to the front of all the lines without anyone complaining. He laughed at the ease at which they cut in front of hundreds of kids at a time.

When we did socialize with others, Jake typically went off on a tirade about how he refused to live like the common man. He explained that he would never live the "suburban nightmare" as he called it. He declared he would never own a minivan and would never have a nine-to-five job like everyone else. Of course, he would say these types of things when we were having dinner or socializing with friends who lived in the suburbs and had typical jobs.

4. REQUIRES EXCESSIVE ADMIRATION, ADULATION, AND ATTENTION

A narcissist always wants to be the center of attention and will do whatever it takes to attract that attention. In conversations, he will often find a way to relate the discussion back to himself. A narcissist needs to be the center of attention at all times. He will wear clothes that are designed to make others notice him. He will spend a fortune on a car as long as it attracts attention. A narcissist will do anything to draw attention to himself.[6]

Andrew

Andrew loved movies. He was so taken by some movie characters that he would emulate their behavior or quote them. Quoting movie lines was a favorite pastime of his. Combining his sense of humor with his wit, he would often throw out movie lines in the middle of conversations. It would confuse some people, but those who understood the relevance found it hilarious. Andrew consumed movies like no one I had ever seen. It can be the ultimate form of escapism for some. He once wrote:

> I wholeheartedly relate to each character, in each movie. Therefore, if it is an action adventure, and some one-dimensional hero saves the day, I feel his strength and courage, his bravery under the threat

of world catastrophe. If a drama, I feel like this victim, this wrongly accused man, this youth misunderstood and confused. But, more profoundly, I feel this connection in love stories, even if the romance is periphery to the story. I see myself as the good-looking leading man, who sweeps the girl off her feet, who charms her with his nodding wink, his glance. More to the point, I see myself as the great lover, the romancer, and the sexual satisfier. I want to be the guy who gets the girl at the end of the story, the man who wins her, who she cherishes. And not only that, but I want that romantic ending when all the players of fate come ready to play, when he says the right thing, when she accepts his apology and takes him back, when, yes, he gets the girl. When he smiles and she smiles—against her best judgment—and they ride off down the holy bond of matrimony.

Unfortunately, what the movies usually fail to explore is what happens when Richard Gere in *Pretty Woman* gets the girl—the hooker— back at his place. What happens in the day to day, after the wedding, the honeymoon, the first house, the first car, what happens when the euphoria is over, and you are left with someone for the rest of your life. How do the movies explain what to do with the time remaining? Movies give me a glimpse. The problem is that movies give me a wholly unrealistic depiction of love, sex, marriage, children, and life together with someone supposedly so special and endearing that one is willing to spend the rest of one's time on earth with this person.

Just so you know, I never saw or read this until after our separation. And no, I didn't go digging for it. He randomly sent it to me. After our separation, Andrew occasionally sent me his writings and poetry. Some of his writings moved me to cry and miss him. Other writings were subtle attempts to crush me.

Jake

Jake liked to pretend to be humble, but secretly sought attention in everything he did. He had to be different than everyone, which drew attention to him. As I mentioned, he owned an RV. He easily could have stored it during the winter and saved it for long distance travel purposes, but that wouldn't bring him the same kind of attention. So he drove his RV all over Chicago, during the cold snowy winters, as it guzzled endless amounts of gas.

It was impossible for people not to notice or comment on it every time we got out of it in the middle of a crowded city street. I remember one time we pulled up outside of a restaurant, which had an outside seating area where many people were dining. In one fell swoop he parked the RV in a space not much larger than a space one would park a car. When we got out of the RV, the entire crowd sitting outside the restaurant stood up and started clapping and cheering for him. Needless to say, he was in his glory.

5. FEELS A SENSE OF ENTITLEMENT

Narcissists do not think that rules and regulations apply to them. They believe they are special and need not conform to society's expectations or laws. They believe typical household chores are beneath them and are insulted at the mere suggestion of performing such mundane tasks. This is what a significant other is for . . . to perform such chores for them.[7]

Andrew

Andrew never lifted a finger around the house. Housework was beneath him. He was too good to put dishes away or take the trash out. Andrew was vehemently opposed to doing any household work. After moving from the city to a home in the suburbs, Andrew would literally look outside our window and make fun of the neighbors for mowing their lawn or landscaping. He would laugh at them and say they needed to get a life.

We got in a huge argument every time the lawn needed to be mowed. I insisted he mow the lawn. This was the one thing I would not back down on. I had picked up every other chore and responsibility in our marriage, including handling our finances, taxes, and so forth. He did absolutely nothing. The one thing I held out on and insisted he do was mow the lawn. However, it was a full-fledged screaming argument every time I asked him to do it. No matter how long the grass got, he refused to mow it without an argument.

There were many things I asked him to do that he never did. I grew so tired of waiting for him to help me around the house that my brother and my dad would often come over to help me with things. I will never forget the day my dad was helping me hang heavy pictures and mirrors throughout our new home while Andrew lay in our bed reading with the door closed. He couldn't be bothered.

Another memorable moment was the day Andrew came home with

a new book he had picked up at the Printers Row book fair in Chicago. My family was over at our house and he couldn't wait to show everyone what would become the newest addition to his expansive book collection. The book he was so proud to show off to us was aptly titled *The Right to be Lazy* by Paul Lafargue.

Jake

Jake felt it was beneath him to adhere to the law. He didn't think he should have to pay taxes to the government like everyone else. He had such a sense of entitlement that he didn't feel the law applied to him. In fact, he hadn't paid taxes for years, and at one point during our relationship, owed the government $30,000 in back taxes. Whenever I confronted him about it, he would get upset and complain about the U.S. government. He would then go on a tirade about how he wanted to move to another country.

6. EXPLOITS OTHERS WITHOUT GUILT OR REMORSE

A narcissist evaluates whether he wants to develop a relationship with someone on the basis of their utility. In other words, how useful a person can be to him is the measure of their worth. He chooses friends based on how well they can help him be noticed or help him become known. This is how a narcissist assesses whether he wants to develop a relationship with someone or not.

A narcissist does not choose his companions based on how much fun he has with them or because he enjoys their company. No, he chooses to develop relationships with only those who are perceived by others to be superior, attractive, or unique in some way. By associating with others who attract attention, he ensures that he will never be deficient in NS. He basically asks himself, "Can this person help make me known?"

Narcissists have absolutely no guilt. They do things without feeling remorse. They are notorious for taking advantage of others, especially their significant other. A classic example of this is the man whose wife puts him through school, and then leaves her the moment he becomes a lawyer or doctor.

Andrew

As I mentioned earlier, Andrew wanted to become a professor. He convinced me that he needed to pursue his studies full time. So instead of bringing in any income whatsoever, he quit his job and pursued his master's degree full time. He moved in with me and I supported us.

While he was in graduate school, he and I got into a terrible fight about something. I was very upset. He responded by telling me he was leaving for the weekend. He was going to stay with his parents because he needed to get away from me. However, before he left me crying on our bed, he grabbed my laptop and said, "Oh, and I'll be taking your laptop with me for the weekend because I have a paper I need to finish for school by Monday."

Jake

Jake had lots of money; however, he never felt he should have to pay full price for anything. Instead, he would scam others out of money. Prior to meeting me, he took two long vacations at premiere resorts practically for free. He was proud of this and liked to brag about it to others.

Basically, he contacted these resorts ahead of time and told them he was a photo-journalist. He even created a fake business card. He told them he was coming to shoot pictures of their resort for an upcoming story in a travel magazine. In response, they put him up in their resort at little to no cost to him and treated him like a king. He felt no remorse about this whatsoever. He was proud of himself and didn't understand why I saw anything wrong with it.

He did this type of thing on a small scale all the time. For example, whenever we would get fast food he would ask for a cup for water and pay nothing for it. However, instead of filling it with water at the soda fountain, he filled it with lemonade or juice.

7. DEVOID OF EMPATHY

A narcissist is not able to put himself in the shoes of another. He is only concerned with his own needs and wants. How to meet these needs consumes him. All of his time and energy is dedicated to the goal of meeting his needs. He is not able to think of another person's needs or feelings, because he only knows how to think about himself. This lack of empathy has often been said to be one of the most visible signs or indicators of pathological narcissism.[8]

Andrew

Andrew and I lived in Chicago for more than six years. Shortly after we were married, Andrew got his first teaching job as a high school history teacher in the suburbs. Andrew commuted from the city to the suburbs by car for the first year. At the end of his first year, he told me he could no longer handle the commute. It was too hard on him. The traffic was beginning to give him such severe road rage that I felt we had to move. He had to drive, and taking the train was not an option based on the schedule and location of where he worked. I decided since I could take the train from the suburbs to my job in the city and walk to work, I would start doing the commute. This is when we moved to the suburbs.

Well, the commute was horrible for me too, but I tried to stay positive. I didn't think it was too much to ask Andrew to drop me off at the train station on his way to work in the morning. The train station was less than five minutes away from the home we bought, and directly on his way to work. Despite this, he considered it a hassle to drop me off every morning. He didn't like the idea of having to wait for me in the morning if I wasn't ready exactly when he wanted to leave. For many months after we moved there, he insisted my parents pick me up and drive me to the train station a few days a week. He used to joke that this "lessened his workload."

My parents lived in the same suburb as us, but on the other side of town. It was completely out of their way to come across town to pick me up and drive me to the train station. It took more than twenty minutes for them to do this, when it took Andrew only thirty seconds to pull over to the train station on his way to work and let me out of the car. My parents had demanding careers and schedules of their own to worry about, and I was an adult. Despite my attempts to explain this to Andrew, he and I argued for months because he insisted that I ask my parents to drive me to the train station half of the week. He would say, "You're their daughter; they shouldn't mind."

Thinking back on it now, I'm actually surprised he never asked me to just jump out of the car as he slowly rolled pass the train station on his way to work. This way he could have preserved more of his precious time.

Jake

Toward the end of my relationship with Jake, I became depressed and suffered from anxiety as I fought back the daunting realization that he was a narcissist. During this time, my faith helped me a great deal. I am not a religious person, but am very spiritual. I had not been to church in years, but wanted to go during this time. I asked Jake to go with me many times. He always refused, so one day I decided I would simply go on my own. Of course, being so controlling, at the last minute he decided to go with me.

Well, I wish he never would have come along. As I was trying to draw strength from the sermon, he sat next to me in the pew and made this impossible to do. Throughout the entire service, he sat and paged through the Bible, sighing and grunting as he earmarked page after page. I finally broke down and asked him what he was doing. He responded, "Oh, I'm just ear-marking every page that mentions rape, pillage, or murder."

This was Jake's sick, sadistic, and controlling attempt to make a mockery of what I was trying to draw strength from. I was barely holding on for dear life, and here my boyfriend, who was supposed to care about me, was aggravating my condition by disrespecting that which was giving me strength.

8. TENDS TO BE ENVIOUS OF OTHERS OR BELIEVES THAT OTHERS ARE ENVIOUS OF HIM

Narcissists refuse to accept that others could be smarter or better than them. Instead of acknowledging this, they convert it into contempt and anger. They are not capable of admiring another person's accomplishments. They believe that others are and should be envious of them.[9]

Andrew

Andrew once wrote about his high school crush and how he tutored her in history. He wrote:

> My approach had to be underhanded. It had to be very understated. She could never know until it was too late, and she was in love with me, that my benign gesture to help her with history was anything other than altruistic, compassionate tutoring. We would make dates—that is, to tutor at the library on Saturday mornings. Cindy was the "it" girl, and of course, as things usually play—this will be cliché, but clichés are clichés for a reason: they were once true—she dated the dumb-headed star football player, whose only attention inside school

was for acting disrespectfully in class and getting the condemnation of the teachers, except in those rare times when teachers found him charming in his infantile ways. Taking attention away from me, I resented him and all the other football players and consistently wished them ill will. Yes, ill will.

Jake

For the longest time, I could not figure out why Jake was so angry and cynical all the time. I finally realized part of this had to do with his seething envy toward others, especially men. He was constantly competing with them.

I remember one time while vacationing in Mexico, he started arguing with a sales manager who was trying to sell us a timeshare. Jake would drag me to timeshare presentations because they offered free lunch, gifts, and discounts on rental cars and hotels. He openly admitted to me that he never had any intention of buying a timeshare, but wanted to take advantage of the free offers and discounts. On one particular occasion, one of the salesmen blatantly called him out on it.

After indulging in a decadent buffet brunch, a salesperson took us around their resort for a tour. He then brought us to his desk to ask some questions about our travel desires and financial situation. When asked if we travel a lot, Jake said yes. When asked if we had money to invest in travel, Jake said yes. Jake basically gave the salesman no good reason why he couldn't buy a timeshare. That is, if that is what we were there to consider doing, but we weren't.

The salesman called his manager over to his desk to close the deal. However, Jake would not budge. He told him he didn't want to invest, but could not give him one good reason why. After an exhausting discourse between the two of them, the sales manager finally became so aggravated that he called Jake out on his game. He said, "I'm sure your girlfriend here has better things to do with her time than have you drag her around to timeshare presentations that you clearly have no serious interest in."

I said nothing and watched Jake respond to the man by saying, "I am a very highly educated man and will not invest in something a man I don't even know is telling me is a good deal."

As the sales manager grew frustrated, Jake egged him on even more by saying, "It's not my fault if you don't like what you do. Get an education so you can get a real job."

9. DISPLAYS ARROGANT AND HAUGHTY BEHAVIOR

Narcissists know how to exhibit false modesty when needed. However, the majority of the time, narcissists are condescending to others. They believe they are far superior to others and are constantly judging others. Their comments are often elitist and haughty.[10]

Andrew

To illustrate this point, below is a poem Andrew once wrote:

Coming out of my cave,
Wandering the streets of a hurried, crowded, yet desolate town,
Listening to the banter of the herd.
They speak, I listen, hearing nothing.
They act, I observe, indignant against their activities.
Fervently waiting for something to happen.
Vitality. Authentic Action. Creative Engagement.
Seeing none, I venture to the mountaintop overlooking
The dissolved remains of a world once exuberant, radiant,
Full of human splendor.

Towering over the valley of mechanical complacency.
I see it all.
The world is before my disillusioned eyes.
You ask, my beloved friend on this sojourn journey,
"What do you see?"
I see so much lethargy, so little life.
A world whose mighty breath is strangled by
The trivialities and regularities of their futile existence.
A people in perpetual fear.
A soul bartering for survival.
Men enslaved for the primal necessities,
Discarding fanciful notions and imaginative inquiries.
Women consumed in the entanglement with domesticity.
All weak, sublimed with mediocrity and falsified Gods.
All sexes, races, peoples mollified with mere existence:
No one living.

You ask excitedly, "What is the way, you wise soothsayer?"

Friend, follow my steps across the scorched ground.
I will lead you to a place
Untarnished by evil, visited by no self-proclaimed saint.
Close your eyes, hold my hand.
Beware of clandestine enticements and subtle diversions
Along the sacred path towards your Awakening.

In this world of precocious endearment, there exists:
Benevolent leaders sincere in actions, gracious with their means.
Study evincing the bounty and wisdom in Learning,
Interpreting the poets, perusing the major voices.
Art lucid in meaning.
Manifesting a congregation of sympathetic will.
Music providing simple quintessential delights
Enriching experience to the most daring level of profundity.

An effusion of joy unable to escape our incessant grasp.
The trees our revered altar,
Water the sanctified blood of eternal youth.
Leaves—green, effervescent, illuminating on a new spring day
They are the jewels to sparkle in the reflection of our eyes.
Bodies to house our fragile souls,
Not to glamorize in frivolous vanity.

Gentleness between lovers, compassion among friends.
Malignant jealously into accommodating respect.
Coarse and tedious conversation becomes
Comfortable and confident silence.

Here, in this imagined world,
No apprehensive laws will restrict your budding individualism.
You will find no religion save Humanism.
You will accept no higher spirit
Except the wondrous harvest of nature.
Here, my comrade in the human condition,
You will witness the regeneration of Man.
Accompany me into this world of unyielding bliss.

Notes

1. Sam Vaknin, *Malignant Self-Love—Narcissism Revisited* (Prague: Narcissus Publications, 2006).
2. Ibid.
3. Ibid.
4. Ibid.
5. Ibid.
6. Ibid.
7. Ibid.
8. Ibid.
9. Ibid.
10. Ibid.

Additional Characteristics of a Narcissist

So we have looked at the criteria or characteristics that help one identify a pathological narcissist as outlined in the DSM. If you will allow me to elaborate, I would like to share some additional signs that helped me finally recognize the pathological narcissism in both Andrew and Jake.

1. HE IS CONTROLLING AND MANIPULATIVE

Being in love with a narcissist is a confusing state of affairs, to say the least. In the beginning, a narcissist makes you feel incredibly loved and valued. He appears to be head-over-heels in love with you and worships the ground you walk on. He writes you poetry, takes you out for romantic dinners, and finds all your little quirks endearing and adorable.

Once a narcissist feels he has obtained control of you (through marriage or moving in together), you will see a completely different side of him that you never knew existed. Narcissists have often been described as having a Dr. Jekyll and Mr. Hyde personality. Once in control, a narcissist becomes demeaning and cruel.

Narcissists are oblivious to others and how their behavior affects people close to them. Unfortunately, this doesn't make their behavior any less hurtful. Narcissists dismiss the feelings, ideas, and opinions of others. They are condescending in their nature. They belittle, criticize, judge, and put others down. They can be blatant about it but are often quite subtle in their approach. They have a way of putting you down in such a way that you don't even realize you have been insulted until you reflect upon the conversation later.

While narcissists are oblivious to the fact that their behavior hurts others, it does not mean that at times, they are not deliberately abusive. A narcissist is purposefully abusive when the relationship with his significant other changes in a way that is not to his liking. An example of this would be when a significant other becomes too close or clingy. Intimacy terrifies a narcissist, and he will respond by being purposefully abusive in order to push the person away.

Another example of when a narcissist would be intentionally abusive is when a significant other voices her displeasure or threatens to leave the relationship. By asserting abusive behavior, a narcissist believes he can maintain his dominance and control over his significant other.[1]

A narcissist has a way of turning everything around so you begin to question yourself. He will do something terribly mean or cruel. You will talk to him about it, but by the end of the conversation, you are the one apologizing for some reason. A narcissist knows how to manipulate better than anyone.

In my experience, a narcissist eventually becomes sarcastic and belittles you constantly. You begin to feel you can do nothing right in his eyes and your presence is hardly tolerable. You're baffled. You wonder what you did wrong to cause such a drastic change in his feelings toward you. You struggle desperately to return things to the way they were in the beginning. Unfortunately, as hard as you try, things will never be the same again. It is a maddening and precarious way to live. It can drive anyone to the edge of their sanity.

Sam Vaknin does an excellent job of describing how a narcissist abuses his victim when he writes:

> "He infiltrates her defenses, shatters her self-confidence, confuses and confounds her, demeans and debases her. He invades her territory, abuses her confidence, exhausts her resources, hurts her loved ones, threatens her stability and security, involves her in his paranoid states of mind, frightens her out of her wits, withholds love and sex from her, prevents satisfaction and causes frustration, humiliates and insults her privately and in public, points out her shortcomings, criticizes her profusely and in a "scientific and objective" manner—and this is a partial

list. Very often, the narcissist acts sadistically in the guise of an enlightened interest in the welfare of his victim. He plays the psychiatrist to her psychopathology (totally dreamt up by him). He acts the guru to her need of guidance, the avuncular or father figure, the teacher, the only true friend, the old and the experienced. All this in order to weaken her defenses and to lay siege to her disintegrating nerves. So subtle and poisonous is the narcissistic variant of sadism that it might well be regarded as the most dangerous of all."[2]

When I did take any real steps at ending either relationship, if verbally abusive behavior did not work to force me into submission, the false self would be the next weapon of defense in their artillery. I think a narcissist believes if his false self worked once to win you over, it will work again to keep you around or win you back.

At this point he will lay on the charm. A narcissist knows when to charm and is sure to remind you that he understands you like no one else can or ever will. It is essential for a narcissist to make you believe only he can understand you. By constantly telling you that you have problems and quirks only he can understand, you start to believe him and begin to feel unlovable in some strange paranoid way.

By telling you he loves you despite your flaws, he hopes you will grow dependent on him. This is a narcissist's way to ensure you will never leave him. It is narcissistic manipulation at its finest.

When a narcissist feels he is in control of you and is not threatened by any fear that you will ask for too much from him or leave the relationship, he will engage in escapist activity and appear as if he hardly notices you exist the majority of the time. You are merely present to dispense secondary NS should his primary NS fail to meet his needs for the day.

When I finally left Andrew, he often asked me during our months of separation to reconsider. He would tell me he couldn't believe I was leaving him. I always responded by saying, "You left this relationship a long time ago." He never did have a response or argument to this for he knew it was true.

Andrew

Andrew had been seeing a therapist. One day, he came home from his therapy session and asked if I would start going with him to see his therapist. He wanted to start couple's therapy. I was surprised by his request, but agreed.

After our first joint visit with his therapist, she gave Andrew a long list of things he needed to do to improve our relationship. When I, in turn, asked what I could do, she responded by saying, "You should be more assertive." This surprised me. I never thought of myself as a doormat.

Narcissists are extremely controlling and manipulative. However, they are very subtle in their approach. They do not start out overly controlling, because they know this is not the way to win your affections. Slowly, over time, they become more and more controlling. You don't even realize it's happening until one day, you wake up and realize he controls every move you make. For some reason, he brainwashes you so well that you're oblivious to his controlling ways until someone points it out to you.

I remember telling my mom that Andrew asked me to start going to couple's therapy with him. I was a little nervous, because up until this point, I had not let on that we had any significant problems. When I told her, I expected her response to be one of total surprise. Instead, she responded by saying, "I am so glad you're going to therapy. I can't believe the way he talks to you. He puts you down and is so controlling. Your father and I have talked about it. If he can talk to you the way he does in front of us, we can't imagine how he talks to you when we're not around."

Jake

Jake criticized me relentlessly for eating meat. We talked about having children together someday, and I asked him what kind of diet we would agree to raise our children on. He said, "Oh, they will most definitely be vegetarian."

I said, "So I will be the only meat eater in the family? That might be confusing for the children. How are we going to explain the difference in my diet to them?"

He responded with a straight face and said, "Oh, we will just tell them that mommy is an animal killer."

Oh sure, I thought, *that won't give the children any nightmares.*

Jake was always judging me. I could never do anything right. Upon returning from a trip to Mexico, which is where I finally ended my relationship with him, I was drinking a diet pop as the plane taxied to the gate. Jake always criticized me for drinking pop because he thought it was unhealthy. Well, he was extremely thirsty so he grabbed my pop without thinking and took a long swig. After he drank out of it, he looked at the label critically and said, "I don't want to think about all the horrible toxic chemicals in here."

I responded by grabbing the pop out of his hand and stating, "And I am so not going to miss being judged by you over a can of pop."

2. He is Obsessed with His Image

The word narcissism is derived from the name Narcissus. Narcissus is the name of a beautiful young male in Greek mythology that refused the love of Echo, the most famous nymph. As punishment for his indifference, he is made to fall in love with his own reflection in a pond of water. Unable to ever physically possess this image, he pines away at the water's edge and eventually turns into the flower that now bears his name—Narcissus.

A narcissist is obsessed with his image and will do whatever it takes to sustain the false self he has created. It is critical to his survival. It protects him from reality and from the threat of experiencing real emotion. Typically, a narcissist will choose to focus on either his talent or looks to get attention, but can swing back and forth between both.

Andrew

Andrew was predominantly a cerebral narcissist. He learned early on that he could use his intelligence to get attention. His somatic narcissism uncovered itself later in our relationship. Years into our marriage, Andrew started to notice that his looks brought him a great deal of attention. He had always focused on his intelligence to gain admiration. However, when he started to notice his looks could get him just as much attention or more, he became obsessed with his physique and started working out at the gym relentlessly. He would spend hours upon hours at the gym. All he could do was talk about his physique.

One of his favorite games was to take a tape measure and pass it around to others so they could measure their arms and determine who had the biggest biceps or "guns," as he liked to refer to them. I can still hear his voice to this very day asking me constantly if I wanted "tickets to his gun show."

During our separation, when we were determining who would take what, Andrew couldn't care less about any of it. Decorating the house was always something I took an interest in, and he scoffed at it as mundane and petty. So I took the initiative to tell him what I wanted, thinking he would object to nothing.

Well, I was wrong about one item. There was one thing he was absolutely adamant about having . . . the large decorative mirror, which hung in our living room. Yes, the same mirror my dad helped me hang while Andrew laid in bed reading. This is what he insisted on having. It was a classic narcissist move. He loved to look at himself as he walked by that mirror every day. He made sure when everything was divided between us, that mirror remained in his possession.

Below is a poem Andrew once wrote, which I believe illustrates his somatic narcissism:

A Man born with a heroic past,
Destined for greatness,
Beset by the calamities of the mind.
Brawn, steel, power.
You see him from afar:
His firm, chiseled jaw protrudes into your vision.
You cannot take your eyes away: his force attracts.
Staring at you, his eyes focused—you cannot escape.
You beg for enslavement, torture.
Any recognition of your being: you need to feel Alive.
His virtues stammer to cessation The eclectic wisdom of tradition.

He looks—no smile, no grin, all you see is strength.
Ferocity of spirit will conquer you—
Do not approach the icy demeanor.
His large, monstrous frame,
Shoulders larger than the settled earth of a thousand mountains.
His body moves, so viral, so potent: Do not get in his way.
Sexual, dangerous, mysterious.
The might of a hundred Caesars pounces on your soul.
You want him to fade subtly into the night,
Absent from the approaching day;
Yet, you do not want the death of his morning touch.

He walks, in a musical melody adorned by the Gods.
Each contouring stride of his body warns
The world of impending danger, of unbridled hope.

People attempt repression;
They threat, they bribe, they maneuver their seduction;
They fail.
He scours his mighty sword
On their enslaved and petty existence,
Slashing all those who impede his progress.
Bowing to none. Questioning all.
Higher and higher he goes.
Faster. Faster.
Moving farther on his own, away from them,
Creating a world fashioned after his heart, his strength,
Affirming his spirit and omnipotence of self.
A place for the cumbersome attachment to fertile emotions.
You do not have a chance.
Be gone, you herd of aggravated conformity.
Der Obermensch has taken his place.

Jake

Jake obtained the majority of his NS from his artwork. This is what brought him the most attention. His art career catered to his cerebral narcissism. However, at the same time, he was sure to utilize his good looks to his advantage as well. While he liked to act humble around strangers, his love affair with himself was undeniable. He was obsessed with his looks.

We traveled a lot and he often used this as an opportunity to get pictures of himself. Wherever we went, he posed and asked me to take pictures of him. Of course, he pretended he had no idea I was taking his picture so it looked like a candid shot. He would take pictures of me and ask that I do the same.

Unfortunately, I was not as good at posing for fake candids as Jake was. He spent the majority of our nineteen day trip through the Greek islands taking pictures. He was so obsessed with getting the perfect photo that it began to frustrate me. I wanted to spend more time taking in the moment and the beauty of it all. We were in a magnificently tranquil and serene place. I didn't want to spend my time taking orders from someone telling me where to stand and how to pose so he could get just the right shot of me.

If the photo didn't turn out to his liking, he would get upset with me.

I remember that more than once he lost it and yelled at me to get that stupid "sorority girl smile" off my face.

He wanted me to act as if I didn't know he was taking my picture so he could get a good candid shot. Now, I know a good candid is a piece of art. However, I will never understand how it is a true candid if you know your picture is being taken. Nevertheless, we would get in argument after argument because my ability to pretend he wasn't taking my picture did not meet his expectations.

Jake, on the other hand, was very good at posing for fake candids. In Cozumel, I had a massage out on the beach under a gazebo. Jake rushed over when my massage was done and used the gazebo as a photo opportunity. He sat on the table with a towel around his neck and asked me to take his picture while he struck a pose.

While vacationing in Tulum, we stayed in a private ocean front villa. There was an outdoor tub on the back deck. He positioned himself in the tub, told me to kneel a few feet behind him and take a picture of him relaxing in the tub looking out onto the ocean. He then propped his arms up on the tub to accentuate his biceps, turned his head to the side so his profile could be seen, and instructed me on how to take his picture.

Narcissists are also concerned with the image their significant other portrays. A narcissist is astutely aware of his significant other's ability to attract attention. In his mind, the more attention she can draw, the more ideal she is to him. You will observe, when with a narcissist, he will always pick up on whether people notice you. If you make him look good or help him get noticed, he eats up every second of it.

3. HE AVOIDS INTIMACY AND SEX

Narcissists dread getting emotionally intimate. They view intimacy as weak. In their mind, becoming intimate with someone cancels their superiority and demystifies them. Also, since intimacy is universally sought, it is perceived as common. As you now know, a narcissist does not feel any common pursuit is worth his precious time. In his mind, if it is common, it can't possibly be worthwhile.

Cerebral narcissists regard sex as a chore . . . something they must do in order to maintain their source of secondary narcissistic supply—their significant other. Somatic narcissists view women as nothing more than sex objects who allow them to obtain narcissistic supply. Beautiful women are particularly attractive to narcissists because they are the ultimate status symbol . . . proof of their masculinity and virility.

Narcissists do not see women in a healthy way. They are unable to appreciate what most men dream of in a woman—someone who is both cute and sexy at the same time. No, narcissists can't help categorizing women into one of two separate categories. For a narcissist, a woman is either cute and sweet (saintly), or sexy (a whore). She can never be both. This is what psychologists refer to as a Madonna-whore complex.[3]

If a woman is sweet and nice, she is classified as a Madonna. If she treats him badly, she is defined as a whore. A Madonna is sexless. A whore turns a narcissist on like nothing else. In the beginning of a relationship, every woman is sexy to a narcissist because the thrill of the chase makes her enticing. The more she plays hard to get, the sexier she becomes. However, once she has been conquered by the narcissist, she slowly loses her desirability. The more comfortable the relationship becomes and the more caring she becomes, the less enticing she is to him sexually. She loses her sex appeal and becomes a saintly Madonna figure.

A Madonna fulfills a narcissist's need to be catered to like a child. A whore fulfills his adult sexual needs. A whore is the only type of woman that turns a narcissist on. A Madonna is completely sexless. Over time, any woman who is good and caring to a narcissist will inevitably become sexless.

Andrew

To illustrate how quickly I changed from an object of desire to a completely sexless being, below is a poem Andrew wrote to me in the beginning half of our relationship.

I penetrate your sanctuary, your holiest domain.
I enter with reserve, fear, need.
You close your eyes; I keep mine open.
Waiting for you to open to the enchantment.
Groping, grabbing, clawing.
Searching for salvation, you scream as a predator of the night.
I want more;
Give me your soul; give me that which is mysterious.
Let my piercing perception uncover the forbidden fruit.
I watch and wait.

Our enmeshed bodies transform
Into a unique, intrinsically human shape.

Beauty no ancient artist could surpass,
Perfect in form, expression, longing.
Your hair sprouts new directions,
Waving, moving, alive with renewed vigor.
Your body moves in passion your mind cannot control.
You scream like a fierce, savage animal.
I watch and wait.

I need you, seek you, cannot live
Without your affectionate touch.

You let go.
Your eyes open.
I see what I came to see.
Your body moves in unchartered territory.
You speak in a native, unrecognizable tongue.
You breathe renewed air—my air.
I look in your eyes: I see into your world:
Dreams, Fears, Desires
Those you hate, those you will always love.
I know your history, your past. I will know your future.
Prudery, propriety, perfection—gone.
Innocence, strength, Eros—ascertained.
You pray for salvation; I answer in acceptance.
We are one—equal in all sacred rights and holy passages.
We are alive—prevented by no force, repressed by no power.
Engaged to the Authority of Copulation.

Years later, Andrew and I were getting ready to enjoy a Friday evening together when he asked if I was menstruating. After confirming I was, he breathed an audible sigh of relief and said, "Good, it's so nice when you have your period because I can relax knowing there's no pressure to have sex with you all weekend."

I will never forget our second therapy session. Andrew turned to his therapist as I sat next to him, holding his hand, and said, "Lisa is my good, sweet wife. I cannot see her sexually or in a sexual way at all. I just see her as my good, sweet Lisa." He basically confirmed that I was completely sexless to him because I was good to him and cared for him.

Andrew's Madonna-whore complex was validated for me again during our separation. We were talking on the phone and he said to me with much enthusiasm, "You know what the main problem in our marriage was?"

I was anxious to hear what he had to say because I thought it might be quite profound. I mean, it sounded like he had given it a lot of thought and had come to a huge realization that he wanted to share with me. So I responded, "What? What do you think our main problem was?"

His response: "You were too nice. You should have been mean to me once in a while. It would have put some fire under my belly."

Basically, he was telling me if I had acted mean or cruel, it would have put the necessary fire under his belt to turn him on. A woman who is kind, sweet, and giving will always be viewed as a saintly, sexless Madonna to a narcissist. Those who act like heartless whores turn him on like nothing else.

Many narcissists revert to pornography at this point, because it portrays women as whores. Pornography is degrading to women, and this is exactly what turns a narcissist on. Many become addicted to pornography.

A narcissist eventually withdraws sexually from any type of intimate relationship you once had with him. I believe it is inevitable in any long-term relationship with a narcissist. You become sexless. You become the Madonna. He still needs you, no doubt. However, this is not because he is in love with you in any adult or mature way. He needs you to continue to cater to his needs. He needs you to ensure that someone will always be present to provide NS, should the outside world fall short of his expectations. He often withholds sex as a form of punishment.

I fear the easy access young teenagers have to pornography today may breed narcissism. When pornography is a teenager's first introduction to sex, I believe it skews their understanding of it. Instead of learning that sex is something you save for someone you love, they see people having sex with many random people in pornography.

What does this tell teens about sex? It tells them that sex is not sacred. It teaches them that sex need not be reserved for only the one you love. Many teens today are learning about sex and love through pornography. As a result, I believe they see the two as mutually exclusive.

In other words, they see sex and love as two completely separate entities, which is precisely how a narcissist views them. A narcissist does not view sex as a reflection of one's love for another. He views sex as something completely separate from love.

To a narcissist, love is sexless, pure, and saintly, whereas sex is dirty and reserved for whores. I remember Andrew would get so upset with me when I referred to sex as making love. He would literally yell at me and say, "No one makes love! Why do people say that? We're not making love. We're not making anything. Do you see anything being made here? I don't. We're having sex. That's all it is."

4. HE CAN'T DESCRIBE LOVE

In the beginning, a narcissist knows how to emulate emotions better than anyone. He knows just what you want to hear, just how to say it, and just how often you want to hear it. He will use this ability of his to ensure you fall madly in love with him. Unfortunately, it is an act. None of it is real. When pressed to describe what love is, you will be surprised by his response. I know I was.

Andrew

Our last fall together, I told Andrew I did not think he was in love with me. He had just been diagnosed with narcissistic personality disorder by the very therapist he asked me to start seeing with him. Based on what I had read about narcissism, I told him narcissists aren't capable of love and I didn't think he loved me. He tried to convince me that he did, and was more than capable of love. We argued back and forth about it for a while. Finally I said, "Okay, then describe love to me. Describe what your love for me feels like."

He gave me a blank stare and paused. I said, "You shouldn't have to think about it that hard."

He quickly responded by saying "My love for you feels like . . . is like . . . well . . . it's like . . . the same warm feeling I get when I look at Abe and Buddy."

Abe and Buddy were our six-year-old cats. I sat in astonishment, for I could hardly believe my husband was describing the love he felt for me by comparing it to the feelings he had for our cats.

The sad thing is, Andrew was being completely honest with me, and

I eventually understood why. By researching narcissism, I learned that narcissists have disconnected from themselves to such a degree that they do not allow themselves to love anyone. It is too risky. It made sense to me that if Andrew were to genuinely care for anyone, it would be someone who posed no threat to him, like our cats.

A pet is a safe haven for a narcissist. A pet poses no threat of abandonment or rejection. A pet offers unconditional love. A pet often follows you around and worships the ground you walk on, right? Well, this is the perfect relationship for a narcissist. A pet will adore and fall all over you, but expects very little in return. That day when Andrew told me his love for me felt the same as when he looked at our cats, my suspicions that he was a narcissist were reconfirmed.

5. HE FINDS NO JOY IN GIVING

Andrew

During our separation, Andrew had many moments of clarity where he openly admitted to me that he felt nothing. One such conversation in particular was when I explained to him that I wanted to be with someone who found joy in giving or doing things for others. I told him I no longer wanted to be with someone who felt it a pain or hassle to do things for me.

Andrew was constantly amazed at my giving nature, and wondered why I gave so openly and freely to others. He wanted to understand from me how I thought I was going to find someone who would enjoy giving to me. I tried to explain why people enjoy giving. I told him that I enjoy giving to others because it makes me happy to see people I care about happy. He gave me a blank and puzzled look and said, "I still don't get it."

I pondered and tried to think of a way to explain it to him so that he might understand. Having just recently learned about his strong feelings for our cats, I decided to use them in my example. I asked him, "How does it make you feel when you share your ice cream with Abe?"

He responded with a huge smile on his face and said, "Oh, it makes me so happy."

I said, "That is precisely the feeling that makes people want to give to others."

He sat in front of me with a look of bewilderment on his face and said, "Wow! That's it? I get it. I actually get it now. I've never felt that before for anyone but our cats. This is the first time I've ever understood why people enjoy doing things for others. I always thought people gave or did things for others just to make themselves look good."

For the next several days, he continued to thank me profusely for helping him feel a feeling he had never experienced before. I am not exaggerating. This was a huge revelation for him. The fact that he was so grateful that I facilitated in him the ability (albeit temporary) to feel a real feeling confirmed his narcissism even more.

In my opinion, narcissists will never let their guard down enough with anyone to ever feel genuine love for them. Therefore, doing things for others whom they have no feelings for is pointless. I think they are able to do this with pets because they pose no threat. Pets will never disagree or intentionally abandon them.

Even their own children pose a threat to them. Children talk back and do not always agree. Narcissists only enjoy being around their children when the child is a shining example or extension of them; or when the child does exactly what the narcissistic parent asks. Since children cannot be on their best behavior 100 percent of the time, I'm sure you can imagine how a narcissistic parent responds to children on a daily basis.

The majority of the time, a narcissist is either jealous of the attention his child receives from his wife or others, or he is frustrated by the amount of time and energy the child requires of him. Since narcissists do not enjoy expending energy or doing things for others unless they get something out of it, they have very little tolerance for the needs and demands of children. There is no immediate gratification for a narcissist after tending to the needs of a child. His whole life is about fulfilling his own needs, not others'.[4]

One Halloween, Andrew didn't want to buy a lot of candy for some reason. I was concerned that we might not have enough to pass out to the trick-or-treaters, but he assured me we would. He typically arrived home from work three or four hours before me. When I returned from work, I asked him if we'd had many trick-or-treaters. He explained that many kids had come by for candy. I was worried and asked if we were running low on candy. He responded by saying, "No, I'm only giving them one piece of candy each. These kids are fat enough as it is and don't need any more candy!"

Jake

I will never forget when Jake was moving his things out after we broke up. In the beginning of our relationship, Jake made paintings for me. The first painting he gave me matched the colors in my place, and I hung it proudly on my living room wall. There were two other paintings he started for me but never finished. I was not completely surprised when I saw that he packed these two unfinished paintings among his things when he was moving out. What did surprise me, however, was what he did after he was done moving everything out.

He came back in one last time, which I thought was to make sure he had not forgotten anything. He scanned the room, looked at the painting he had made for me, looked at me, and then proceeded to march directly up to the painting and rip it down off the wall in a huff. He stormed off with it and slammed the door behind him like a five-year-old child.

Several weeks later, after trying to win me back because he could not stand the fact that he could no longer control me, he emailed me to tell me he had just joined an online dating service. I guess this was supposed to make me jealous. He told me to check out his profile. Upon looking it up on the Internet, I found that he had posted a picture of himself standing next to the very painting he had given me and then taken back. The painting that hung on my wall for over a year with no frame, just the canvas, was now beautifully framed as he stood next to it and posed for his online dating picture.

This was obviously an attempt to hurt me. All it did was reinforce his narcissism even more. I downloaded and saved that picture to be sure I never forget how cruel he can be.

6. HE ACTS AS IF YOU DO NOT EXIST

Andrew

Our last summer together, Andrew and I went to visit my college friends, Amy and Doug, in New York for a weekend. One night during our visit, we went out to dinner with a group of people, most of whom we knew and a few we had just met that night. Andrew really hit it off with Patrick, who worked for the New York Public Library. He was quite the intellectual and he and Andrew had a field day together, displaying their intelligence to one another. We left dinner and met a larger group of people at a bar nearby.

As I proceeded to drink more and more at the bar, I suddenly stopped and noticed the situation I was in. I realized that for the past hour I had been talking to two attractive single men who worked with Doug. Upon realizing this, I began to feel guilty for my flirtatiousness. I turned to look for Andrew. He was standing in the corner, laughing it up with Patrick, completely unaware of where I was or what I was doing.

The group then decided to leave the bar to go to a party. We needed more than one cab. We walked outside to get into a couple cabs that pulled up for us. I followed Andrew to get into the cab he was getting in, and he turned to me, stopped me, and pointed at the cab in front of us. He said, "No, go and get in that cab up there." I turned instinctively and proceeded to follow his instructions.

There were only two people in the cab I got in, so there was plenty of room. However, the two people in the cab were the two single men I had felt guilty for flirting with earlier. As I got in they both looked at each other oddly and then looked back at me and asked, "What are you doing?" I responded by explaining that Andrew had told me to get into their cab. They both looked at me with a confused stare and turned around to see what Andrew was doing getting into a different cab. It was humiliating. Andrew was so absorbed in his conversation with Patrick, I might as well have been invisible.

That fall, Andrew and I started talking about having children. I was thirty at the time. We agreed that we would seriously start trying to get pregnant at the beginning of the new year. Before that happened, I went back to New York to visit Amy. It was to be a girls' weekend. Every year in October, my friend Tara and I visit Amy in New York to celebrate her birthday with her. We spend the weekend doing girl stuff.

That year, on the night of Amy's birthday party, her husband made arrangements for bottle service at one of New York's hottest bars. Many of his work friends were there, including one of the two I had shared a cab with during my last visit. His name was Mark. As everyone continued to drink more and more, Mark and I started dancing together.

Hours and drinks later, I found myself telling Mark all about the problems in my marriage. I told him how I had spent years trying to fix things, only to find that things were getting worse in my marriage, not better. It was the first time I had spoken out loud to anyone besides my mother about the problems in my marriage.

I look back and believe that at this time I intentionally (albeit subconsciously) forced myself to face reality before Andrew and I had children together. I could handle the mental anguish that our relationship caused me. However, I could not and would not ever expose my children to the same type of abuse. We were fighting constantly at this point, and to subject children to this would have been cruel and selfish.

I know I did not come to this realization in the best way possible. I poured all of my feelings and problems out to a complete stranger—a man I didn't even know, but thought I could trust because he was a friend of a friend. I hadn't even told my girlfriends the struggles Andrew and I were having at this point.

I believe by interacting with Mark the way I did that evening, I forced the realization upon myself that I had to look at my marriage honestly. I talked to Mark most of the night. He listened with compassion and empathy, telling me stories of his own heartache. We danced together for hours. When the bar closed, the party moved to someone's home. When we got there, I found an empty room and sat in the dark, my head reeling from what I had just shared with Mark.

After some fresh air, I knew enough to remove myself from the situation and stay away from Mark. So I waited alone in the dark in this empty room until Amy and Doug were ready to go home. When they were, they came to get me. I was staying at their place and sleeping on their couch.

As the three of us started to leave the party to get a cab, Mark asked Doug if he could come back to their place so we could continue partying. Doug told Mark we were done partying, but Mark got in the cab with us anyway. The four of us got back to Amy and Doug's place and they went to bed immediately.

Mark and I sat on the couch and continued to talk. He had his arms around me and was playing with my hair. I had been starved of affection for years. The warmth he showed me was so foreign it felt wonderful. He tried to kiss me many times. I avoided each attempt, but there was no denying at one point, our lips touched and his hands lay on my body in an inappropriate way as I fell asleep in his arms on the couch.

I woke in the morning and left for the airport right away as I had an early flight home. Andrew was there to pick me up at the airport. When I got in the car, I burst into tears, telling him what had happened with Mark. I apologized profusely. He responded by yelling at me loudly for a few minutes and then said, "It's okay, what do you want to eat for lunch?"

That was it. He was over it and didn't want to talk about it anymore.

I felt so grateful to have a husband who was so forgiving and understanding. For days, I thought he was such a wonderful man for forgiving me like that. Then, a few days later, after giving it some more thought, my view on everything changed.

7. HE ESCAPES OR DISAPPEARS

Andrew

I told my mom what happened in New York with Mark and how Andrew responded. She knew how grateful I was that Andrew forgave me. She was aware that we were having problems because I had told her a few weeks prior that Andrew had asked me to begin couple's therapy with him.

So a few days after I returned from my trip, my mom and I were working out together at the gym. After our workout, I began telling my mom that the feeling of gratitude I had for Andrew's forgiveness was starting to fade. It was being replaced by a different feeling, a feeling that gnawed at me. I realized that I never would have allowed what happened in New York with Mark to happen if my marriage were a happy one. I realized that recent events prohibited me from ignoring the problems in my marriage any longer. I could no longer deny it. I had to face reality.

My mom agreed that I needed to look at things between Andrew and me. She then pointed out that Andrew engaged in numerous escapist activities. He went to the movies alone, read constantly, slept all the time, and recently had been spending hours a day at the gym. She asked what I thought he was escaping from.

While I did not know what he was escaping from, I knew he was attempting to escape from something. There was something making him terribly unhappy, and he used multiple methods of distraction to avoid it. I went home that night with a mission in mind. I was going to find out what he was escaping from.

I confronted him about it, and he explained that he often had deep thoughts he needed to escape from. I asked him what kind of thoughts he was having. He proceeded to explain by saying, "Sometimes after dropping you off at the train station in the morning on my way to work, I fantasize about what it would be like if I just kept driving."

I asked him, "Drive where?"

"I don't know where. Just drive. I often wonder what would happen if I just kept driving."

I asked again, "Drive where?"

Growing frustrated, he responded again, "I don't know where . . . I just wonder what would happen if I did!"

It was clear that he was fantasizing about leaving me and the life we had together. What he had been escaping from all this time was the reality of his life with me in the suburbs. A narcissist is terrified of living a boring, mundane existence. Domestic life is his worst nightmare. He was miserable in our marriage and fantasized about leaving me.

As I tried to process what he was telling me, he said, "I have deep thoughts about many things, such as life, war, and religion that you don't know about."

I responded, "I had no idea you have such disturbing thoughts you need to escape from." He then said, "Well, if you showed more interest in what I read, perhaps you would recognize this."

That evening I committed to make more of an effort to notice what Andrew read. Andrew was always reading. He read very esoteric books. In the beginning of our relationship, this impressed and fascinated me. I loved hearing about what he read. However, over time and after having enough of my own reading to do when I attended graduate school, I lost some interest in what he read. I never knew this bothered him, but of course it would. He wanted me to be fascinated by his brilliant mind. That night, as we went to bed, I laid my head on his chest and read what he was reading.

He was reading Christopher Lasch's book, *The Culture of Narcissism in an Age of Diminishing Expectations*. Lasch's book, first published in 1978, supported the belief that the Western civilization has become increasingly narcissistic. I read one paragraph and realized that I needed to explore the true meaning of narcissism. Andrew had always joked about being a narcissist, but I never took it as anything serious. I just thought it meant he was overly confident and self-absorbed at times, which anyone could see. I didn't realize the true implications of narcissism. I still do not think many people do.

The next morning, I typed narcissism into an Internet search engine. What I learned changed my life. My mouth was practically on the floor as I read and learned how pathological narcissism manifests itself in a relationship. As I read the description of a narcissist, I was amazed. It described Andrew perfectly. The most helpful website was Sam Vaknin's website, http://malignantselflove.tripod.com. It provided examples of what a narcissist would say and it seemed as if the examples were literally quoting Andrew.

One example that really hit home explained the view narcissists hold on having children. It explained that narcissists often refer to breeding, or having children, as a common pursuit, not to be highly valued. Anything common or easily obtained by many is of no value to a narcissist. I sat in shock, terror, and relief, as I finally understood the man who had confounded and eluded me for years.

That same day, we were scheduled for our third appointment with his therapist. As we drove together to therapy, I said nothing about what I had learned that day on the Internet. We sat in session with his therapist and talked about what happened between Mark and me in New York the weekend prior.

I could tell his therapist was surprised by how unaffected Andrew was by what happened. She wanted to explore this and asked him about it. He had no response. Then she said to him, "Andrew, do you think you're not bothered by what happened between Lisa and Mark because of your Madonna-whore complex? Are you actually turned on by the fact that Lisa was a bad girl?"

I sat and waited with bated breath as he pondered her question. He finally responded to her in a very matter-of-fact tone and said, "Yes."

When it was finally my turn to talk about how I was feeling, I unleashed what I had learned that day about narcissism. Andrew's therapist looked at him bewildered and said, "Andrew, I'm surprised this is the first time Lisa is learning about narcissism, since you and I talk about it so frequently in our sessions."

I told her that Andrew had always joked about being narcissistic, but I took it as nothing more than confirmation that he was overly confident. I did not fully understand pathological narcissism until I researched it that day on the Internet. She then suggested that for our next visit, she meet with me alone, since I was trying to digest so much at the time and seemed very overwhelmed.

The next week was long and excruciating. I told Andrew he was incapable of love and didn't love me. He tried to lay on the charm and convince me that he loved me. However, this time his act did not work on me. Once I understood the true meaning of narcissism, it was as if a mask had been lifted from his face. Everything he said to me after that was so fake and contrived. Nothing he said seemed real, and he showed no emotion toward me as I contemplated divorce. Believe me, I searched his face and waited patiently, hoping he would give me one reason to stay.

One time during that week I saw his eyes fill with tears. I actually had a glimmer of hope, thinking he might have real emotions for me. I quickly asked, "What's wrong?"

He responded, "Do you know who T.S. Eliot is?" I answered, "Yes, he's a writer." "Exactly, he wrote the poem 'The Hollow Men.' It is a great poem." I said, "Okay, yes?"

He continued, "Well, T.S. Eliot was brilliant and misunderstood, just like me, but his wife didn't leave him. No, she stayed by his side. She went into an insane asylum, but she never gave up on him. You don't understand me and never will. No one understands me." He continued to explain that it was not his fault if others were too ordinary or common to understand his complexity and depth.

While I initially thought Andrew was experiencing some type of real emotion over the thought of losing me, what he was experiencing was a narcissistic injury. His emotions had nothing to do with me. They were all about him and his ego. I sat in astonishment as I witnessed the behavior of a textbook narcissist.

Days later, it was time for me to see his therapist alone. At the beginning of our session, I asked her, "Andrew has Narcissistic Personality Disorder, doesn't he?"

She looked at me, paused, nodded her head, and said under her breath but loud enough for me to hear, "Most definitely," and then proceeded to tell me, "I don't like putting labels on people, but yes, Andrew has NPD."

I asked her if she thought our marriage had a chance and if I should continue to try to fix things between us. She explained that NPD is a personality disorder, such as borderline personality disorder and someone with such a problem can rarely be changed. She said the best we could do is continue meeting with her as we had been, and she could tell him what he needed to do to appear more caring and compassionate.

I wasn't ready to give up and did a great deal of research on the topic. I found a therapist who was an expert in personality disorders and wrote her dissertation on narcissism. Instead of proving Andrew's therapist wrong, she confirmed all of my fears. A personality disorder, such as NPD, is a pattern of behavior that begins in childhood. Unlike other behaviors that can be modified, the behaviors of someone with a personality disorder are part of his or her character or personality. This means he or she cannot change, and if you desire to continue the relationship with this person, you will need to make the changes necessary to take better care of yourself.[5]

I realized I could no longer be with someone who was simply acting out emotions to maintain the status quo. I could no longer live a lie. I wanted the real thing. I wanted to be with someone who genuinely loved me for me and found joy in making me happy because he wanted to, not because he was being instructed on how to do so by a therapist. This is when I decided I could choose to live my life in a loveless marriage with someone I knew was incapable of change, or take the steps necessary to re-create my life and move on. It was at this point I made the difficult decision to file for divorce.

A narcissist's biggest fear is that he will find himself in a mediocre existence. He feels omnipotent, grandiose, and unique. To live a routine, common life terrifies him. Andrew was bored with our life in the suburbs. He subconsciously brought about the demise of our relationship. He wanted me to leave him so that he would no longer live a life of monotony.

A narcissist has a lot of built-up resentment toward his significant other for many reasons. First, he knows he is reliant on her for NS. Second, he blames her for tying him down to a boring and mundane lifestyle. This creates in him a great deal of anger toward her. He does not want to rely on her, but knows he has to in order to sustain his false existence. He doesn't respect her, because he knows she puts up with a lot of abuse from him. She has done nothing wrong but be overly giving and nurturing. Yet he is angry with her and blames her for all of his unhappiness.

Most likely, he will never leave, because he cannot risk a break in his NS. Instead, he will continually withdraw from his significant other or degrade her until it gets to the point that she cannot handle the devaluation anymore and leaves him.[6]

This is how my marriage to Andrew ended. Not surprisingly, this is exactly how my relationship with Jake ended as well.

Jake

I thought I had learned so much from my relationship with Andrew that I would never allow myself to be fooled by a narcissist again. I was so sure of it. I can't remember how many times I told people that Jake was the polar opposite of Andrew. I was so certain he was the furthest thing from a narcissist in the beginning that when his true colors started to show, I refused to acknowledge them.

One time toward the end of our relationship, as Jake and I talked about our future and thought of names for our children, as we had done before, he turned to me and said, "I'm not sure if I want to have children after all. They will just tie us down, you know. There's nothing that special about having kids anyway. I mean, anyone can do it. Breeding is common."

There were those three words again: "breeding is common." They were the exact same words Andrew had used when describing his thoughts on having children with me. I could barely speak after he said these words to me. I did not know how to respond.

Shortly after this, Jake and I went to Cozumel for my friend Tara's wedding. We arrived on a Wednesday, and the wedding was on Saturday. The first day we all went down to the oceanfront to lounge, get some sun, and catch up with one another. Someone was smoking a cigarette, which Jake did not approve of at all. He kept waving his hand in front of his face and was so obnoxious that at one point, he got up and moved several lounge chairs away, where no one was sitting. When I yelled over to ask him what he was doing, he responded by shouting back, "I can't sit in that filthy smoke. It's disgusting."

That first day was the only time he sat with me on the beach during our entire trip. Once he found the dive shop, he was scuba diving every day. Sometimes he went on two or three trips a day. My friends were always asking where he was, and I simply responded every time, "Oh, he's scuba diving again."

One day, Tara suggested I take scuba diving lessons so I could spend more time with him. Seeing as how that was all he had any interest in doing, I thought it might be a good idea for me to learn.

I thought by learning something Jake was passionate about it might bring us closer. So I signed up for lessons and couldn't wait to tell him. When I finally saw him later that day after all his diving trips and told him I was going to take a lesson, he responded by looking at me oddly and asking "Why would you do that?"

That night, as we went to bed, I told him I was setting the alarm early because my scuba lesson at the pool was scheduled for 9:00 am. He responded by telling me that he needed me to set the alarm even earlier because he was going on a scuba diving trip of his own at 8:30 that morning. I didn't say anything, but I was disappointed he wasn't going to join me for my first lesson. I shrugged it off and thought *at least he'll be back in time for the second half of my lesson,* which was scheduled for noon. The second half of my lesson was going to be in the ocean, and I really wanted him there.

Well, I went to my 9:00 AM lesson at the pool. There were about five people there for the lesson. Before we could get in the pool for our lesson, we had to answer some basic questions about our medical history and health. I completed my questionnaire and gave it to the instructor. A few minutes later, she pulled me aside, away from everyone, and told me I had failed the questionnaire.

She gave me a new form and told me how to answer each question correctly so that I would pass the test and be able to scuba dive that day. Nice, huh? They just want your money. Your safety is their last concern.

My instructor was female, and even though it was a short lesson, I felt some comfort knowing she had an idea of my strengths and weaknesses for the more difficult lesson later that day in the ocean. You see, I never really learned how to swim as a child. I can get by and tread water fairly well, but have no experience swimming long distances. I had ear problems as a child—four sets of tubes and a ruptured eardrum. Although I tried to take swimming lessons a few times, I could never be in the water long enough to really learn how to swim or take advanced lessons.

When I showed up at the oceanfront for my lesson at noon, the female instructor we had that morning was nowhere to be found. We now had a different instructor. He was a man I had never seen before. He was impatient and rude. He rushed all of us down to the oceanfront, yelling at us for moving too slow. Not only was the instructor different, but there was no Jake. Jake had not yet returned from his morning dive.

There were eight or nine people in this lesson, and they were not the same people from the lesson that morning in the pool. A couple of people were the same, but that was it. As we stood at the oceanfront, I noticed the instructor did not assign any of us a buddy. I knew from Jake's countless scuba diving adventure stories that every time you dive (even if you are advanced) you are assigned a buddy. The buddies are responsible for keeping track of one another underwater.

I was about to ask the instructor when he was going to assign buddies, but before I could, he abruptly instructed us all to dive in and begin swimming out into the ocean. We were about two hundred to three hundred feet out when I began to notice there was water in my mask. What I didn't realize at the time was that there was a hole in it. I went to the surface to empty the water and readjust my mask, but this obviously didn't help. I was up and down a few times fooling with my mask like this, trying to keep water from seeping in.

Finally, I told myself to forget it and go find the group before they got too far ahead of me. Since the instructor never assigned buddies to us, I had no idea if anyone noticed when I went to the surface. I readjusted my mask one last time and plunged deep below. As I tried to stabilize my breathing and rejoin the group, my heart was pounding in hopeful anticipation that they had waited for me. I kept swimming deeper, hoping to see the rest of the group at any moment. Only, I saw no one. I swam faster and deeper, but still . . . no one. I finally realized I was alone.

I tried to stay calm, but water continued to fill my mask, making it difficult to breathe. I was at the bottom of the ocean and could find no sign of human life anywhere. I started to panic. At that point, I desperately needed air. I swam to the top of the water, ripped my mask off and started screaming for help.

There was a boat in the distance. I thought I heard someone from the boat yell back, "Hold on, someone's coming," but I could barely hear. The weight of the scuba tank kept pulling me down under the water. I couldn't keep my head above water to hear or breathe. I had to use all the might in my legs, kicking frantically, just to get my head above the surface for a gasp of air.

My breath was getting weak. I started to hyperventilate. The weight of the tank was beginning to overpower my physical strength.

I could no longer pull myself fully above the water to get any air. Instead I got my head halfway above the surface and swallowed water every time I tried. At this point, I was drowning.

All of a sudden, someone grabbed me from behind, pulled me toward him, and held me above the water so I could breathe. As I caught my breath and began to focus, I looked into the eyes of a stranger. He was a stranger, but his eyes seemed familiar. He had my grandma's eyes. I had never seen anyone with eyes like hers before, and here saving me was a man with her eyes. I felt her presence. He was like an angel.

As he swam me toward safety and we approached the boat, someone threw a line out for me to grab. I grabbed it and was pulled toward the boat. A hand reached down from the boat to lift me up. As I went to grab the extended hand, I recognized it. I looked up and shuddered when I saw who it was. It was Jake.

I couldn't believe it. There was Jake, standing on the side of the boat, watching me drown. The man I was in love with and planning to spend the rest of my life with had stayed on the boat while another man—a complete stranger—jumped in and risked his life for me. I asked Jake later if he knew I was the one drowning and he said, "Yes, I'm the one who first heard your scream for help. I recognized your voice right away."

I don't think Jake thought once to jump in that water and save me. As I grabbed his hand, he pulled me up onto the boat. I buried my head in his chest and cried, waiting for him to console me. Instead, he pushed me away and attacked me with questions: "What were you doing? How could you let that happen? Did you drop your tank? Why didn't you drop your tank? Did you inflate your vest? Why didn't you inflate your vest? I knew you shouldn't have tried to scuba dive. I knew you couldn't do it. It requires common sense, and you don't have any."

He was so cruel that it was becoming obvious to others that I needed consoling. Several strangers came over to me and rubbed my arm to ask if I was okay. Jake just stood there, refusing to comfort me and continuing to question me on every decision I had made in the water.

What I eventually realized was that Jake was embarrassed. Jake always prided himself on being an extreme sportsman. He had his own scuba gear that he traveled with when he vacationed. He liked to think others viewed him as a talented and athletic sportsman. He had been scuba diving with these people all week. He was mortified when his virile image was diminished by his drowning girlfriend, who couldn't even complete a scuba diving lesson.

As we got off the boat, I pointed at my instructor and identified him for Jake. I marched right up to my instructor and asked him how he could leave me behind like that. I turned to my side, thinking Jake was next to me, backing me up, but he wasn't. I looked in the distance and saw him taking off his wet suit by the dive shop, completely ignoring me. I was in utter disbelief. I fought back my tears and started to walk away, hoping to find some of my girlfriends. As I turned away, I heard him yell, "Lisa, where are you going?" I looked over at him and he used his head to motion me over to him.

I approached him, still shaking, and said, "I really just need you to hold me right now. It will help me stop shaking. Can you please do that for me?"

He snapped back at me and said, "I have to put my dive equipment away. Can't you see that? I can't just leave it here. Can you understand that? Go sit down and give me a few minutes."

I did an about-face and walked toward my friends, who were sunbathing on the shore. I tried to sit down, but instead burst into tears as I bent down to grab my towel. So I just kept walking and proceeded to our hotel room.

On the way to our hotel room, I saw Paige, from the wedding party, and she asked me what was wrong. I had to tell her something, for she saw me crying. I quickly told her that I had almost drowned and Jake was being insensitive. I told her I just wanted to be alone. She was the only person I said anything to, and that's all I shared with her.

Jake came back to the room and yelled at me some more for not knowing better to drop my tank or inflate my vest. I explained to him that he wasn't helping the situation and that all I wanted was for him to hold me and comfort me. I was still shaking. I was pleading for empathy. I was begging for it.

But he could not give it to me. He could not reach out to me and simply hold me. Instead, as a typical narcissist, he was more concerned about what others thought of him. He didn't know if I told anyone what had just happened, but he had to find out. Instead of just asking me, however, he tricked me into telling him I told someone.

He said, "Why did you have to tell your friends what happened?"

I responded, "I didn't . . . I only told Paige because I ran into her while I was on the way back to our room and she saw that I was crying. She asked me what was wrong and all I told her was—"

Before I could finish explaining, he exploded, "So you *did* tell your friends? That's just great! Now I have to spend the rest of the week with these people who think I'm a horrible boyfriend! Thanks a lot! Do you know how awkward I'm going to feel around them now?"

He was embarrassed again. In classic narcissist fashion, he was more concerned with how this event affected his image among my friends. Not once did he consider my feelings. He was embarrassed on the boat because it ruined his image as an avid sportsman. He was embarrassed again in front of my friends because he didn't want to look like a bad boyfriend.

Not once did he care that I was still shaking uncontrollably. Instead of helping me calm down, he became more enraged and continued to berate me for all the mistakes I had made while scuba diving. He then said, "You are a total drama queen! You created this whole event just to get attention. I can't believe I'm with such a drama queen," and stormed out of the hotel room, slamming the door behind him.

I stayed in the hotel room and comforted myself. When I finally calmed down and was presentable again, I walked down to the ocean-front to get something to eat and drink. I sat by myself and watched Jake pace back and forth between the dive shop and the boat on the shore. I couldn't believe it, but it looked as if he was going to go on another dive. He saw me sitting there watching him and, sure enough, he got on the boat and took off for another three-to-four hour scuba dive.

Jake was doing the same thing Andrew had. As our relationship progressed and we talked more and more about settling down together, Jake pulled back and retreated. He was terrified of a life of domesticity with me. The closer we came to making a commitment, the more he retreated. He spent his days talking about another life and his nights dreaming of another life by perusing the Internet for hours. He was pushing me away by becoming increasingly insensitive and cruel. He was judgmental and critical of everything I did.

He wanted me to leave him, and the scuba diving incident is what finally pushed me over the edge to end it. I finally gave him what he wanted. I could take no more. Not to mention, I could never look at him the same after realizing he had stood at the edge of the boat and done nothing as I screamed for help that day.

When he returned from his dive, I told him it was over. His response? "Phew, the burden has been lifted. Good luck finding someone who will put up with you."

Notes

1. Barbara Engel, *The Jekyll and Hyde Syndrome*, (Hoboken, NJ: John Wiley & Sons, Inc., 2007).
2. Sam Vaknin, *Malignant Self-Love—Narcissism Revisited*, (Prague: Narcissus Publications, 2006).
3. Ibid.
4. Ibid.
5. Engel, *The Jekyll and Hyde Syndrome*,
6. Vaknin, *Malignant Self-Love*,

Why You Fall For Him

So why do we fall in love with them in the first place? Remember, in the beginning, narcissists appear overly compassionate and caring. They portray a false modesty that prevents us from seeing their true colors.

Sure, there are narcissists who aren't as good at hiding their selfishness as others. They are not as successful in life. Those who are good enough actors to hide their elitism, or at least be more subtle about it, have the most success in manipulating others. These narcissists succeed in winning our love. A smart narcissist will surely win your love, but on a false pretense. He presents himself in a manner he knows will fulfill all your fantasies.

Unfortunately, once you have committed to him, he no longer maintains the image of himself you fell in love with initially. You wonder what happened to the caring and wonderful man you fell for, and try to figure out what you did wrong to make things go so awry.

You must remember, you did nothing wrong. Do not be mad at yourself for being fooled. A narcissist is fun and charismatic. It's very difficult to escape his charm. He can seduce almost anyone. He pretends to be overly caring and compassionate in the beginning, but it is an act. He presents a false modesty that anyone would believe. Unfortunately, this ability to fake modesty has become less of a required skill in today's society.

The star of one of the most-watched television shows in America, Simon Cowell, acts like a complete narcissist. For some reason, our society finds his cruel and demeaning behavior entertaining. He rips apart the fragile psyches of teenagers and young adults with absolutely no remorse and we find this a pleasurable form of entertainment. Instead of being disgusted by it, we make it the number-one show in America! Not only that, but we allow our youth to perceive the attainment of fame as the ultimate measure of success in life. It is this reinforcement of narcissism by society that validates and encourages such behavior.

I wish the media would stop reporting on the lives of people I have no reason to revere. I do not admire people who exhibit selfish, arrogant, and cruel behavior, nor do I wish to hear about them. They set a horrible example for our youth.

I long for the days when journalism involved real investigative reporting on topics that impact our world. I want to return to a society that pays attention to real issues, such as the war, the economy, foreign relations, education, the environment, health care reform, poverty, and gun control. Instead, we pretend these issues do not exist. Talking about politics at work or dinner is perceived as taboo, but analyzing whether Paris Hilton should go to jail is more socially acceptable? I just don't get it.

In Al Gore's book, *The Assault on Reason*, he points out the fact that the media attempts to divert our attention away from real issues by bombarding us with stories about Britney Spears, Lindsay Lohan, and Jessica Simpson. In order for democracy to flourish, we need a free and courageous press, not one that hides behind sensationalism.[1]

While it is clear our society reinforces narcissistic behavior in many ways, I feel that creating awareness of this problem is essential. I believe it is a growing social and psychological problem we can no longer afford to ignore.

Famous historian, Daniel J. Boorstin, once said on the topic, "As individuals and as a nation, we now suffer from social narcissism. The beloved Echo of our ancestors, the virgin America, has been abandoned. We have fallen in love with our own image, with images of our making, which turn out to be images of ourselves."

I have to believe America will restore its glory, but only if we begin to talk honestly about real issues. I am hopeful and believe President Obama will return us to a society that values democracy and engages in real dialogue about real issues. At one time, this country was renowned for its progress in science and technology. We put the first man on the moon. Our last president knowingly censored NASA scientists who tried to educate the world on global warming.

If we return to a country that leads the world on issues of importance

to everyone, we will return to a nation of greatness. Fortunate'
have a President who respects our Constitution and remember.
of Abraham Lincoln in his famous Gettysburg Address: "that government
of the people, by the people, and for the people shall not perish from the
earth."

Notes
1. Al Gore, *The Assault on Reason*, (New York: Penguin Press, 2007).

Why He Does It

While today's celebrity-focused, reality television world certainly encourages and rewards narcissistic behavior, it is important for us to be mindful of another dynamic at play here. This problem has been around since the beginning of time and is certainly not new to our society.

The British Prime Minister from 1766 to 1778, William Pitt, said in a speech to the UK House of Lords in 1770, "Unlimited power is apt to corrupt the minds of those who possess it."

What happened when the government deregulated certain industries and gave CEOs more power than they should have? They abused their power, didn't they? With few checks and balances in place, they took advantage of a system that allowed them to make themselves richer, regardless of how this impacted others. Greed and corruption took over. Morals were thrown out the window in the ever-increasing thirst for profit. Abuse of power was no longer checked by any threat of negative repercussions.

Does absolute power corrupt absolutely? As is often said, the true measure of one's morals is what one does when no one is looking. I believe it is safe to say that power can corrupt one's mind. However, why is it that power corrupts the minds of some while others are able to escape its negative influence?

In my opinion, the ability to avoid the corruption of power is dependent on the ability to self-reflect. Individuals who are put in positions of authority are given great latitude. Incompetent leaders can easily assign blame to others working underneath them. Shifting the blame like this is something we see all too often in Corporate America. By doing this, your supervisor avoids responsibility for any work seen as subpar, but will quickly take credit for any work perceived as exemplary, right?

People in positions of power have many opportunities to demean and hurt others financially while boosting his own image and bank account. What has always baffled me, however, is how these people sleep at night. I believe they do this by disconnecting from themselves. In my opinion, disconnecting is the only way they can blame others for failings and take credit for successes with no remorse. Refusing to self-reflect allows them to stay in the dark and pretend they are not abusing their power.

If they are in touch with their true selves, they are aware of their feelings. Feelings such as fear, guilt, or anger can get in the way of making certain decisions. People who have the ability to self-reflect and look inwardly at their behavior can recognize when they are acting out of fear or jealousy. As a result, they are able to pause and correct their behavior, thereby ensuring they do not allow their own insecurity to get in the way of doing what is right.

Unfortunately, not everyone has the ability to self-reflect. As you know, narcissists are not in touch with their true selves. Therefore, they do not have the capacity for self-reflection. Without the aptitude to look inward, narcissists will blame everyone else for the failings in their lives and criticize others relentlessly. Please understand this criticism is simply a projection, for a narcissist is never truly happy with his life. He feels like a fraud and envies those who are in touch with themselves. A narcissist will never admit when he is wrong.

This temptation to exercise unrighteous dominion exists in any situation where one is in a position of power or influence. It can occur at school, work, church, your community, and in homes and families. A man who practices unrighteous dominion in his home single-handedly destroys the self-esteem of his wife and children. He may not even realize he is abusing his power, but simply knows no other way to behave.

In an effort to avoid such unnecessary abuse, we need to build awareness of this growing problem and find ways to help others get in touch with their true selves. Decisions must be made with full consciousness, and people must take personal responsibility for their actions.

According to the scriptures, a righteous man of power is one who presides:

- *By persuasion:* He uses no demeaning words or behavior, does not manipulate others, appeals to the best in everyone, and respects the dignity and agency of all humankind—men, women, boys, and girls.

- *By long-suffering:* He waits when necessary and listens to the humblest or youngest person. He is tolerant of the ideas of others and avoids quick judgments and anger.
- *By gentleness:* He uses a smile more often than a frown. He is not gruff, loud, or frightening; he does not discipline in anger.
- *By meekness:* He is not puffed up, does not dominate conversations, and is willing to conform his will to the will of God.
- *By love unfeigned:* He does not pretend. He is sincere, giving honest love without reservation even when others are unlovable.
- *By kindness:* He practices courtesy and thoughtfulness in little things as well as in the more obvious things.
- *By pure knowledge:* He avoids half-truths and seeks to be empathetic.
- *Without hypocrisy:* He practices the principles he teaches. He knows he is not always right and is willing to admit his mistakes and say "I'm sorry."
- *Without guile:* He is not sly or crafty in his dealings with others, but is honest and authentic when describing his feelings.

Moving On

Deep down, Andrew and Jake are good people who would never intentionally harm anyone. While they certainly know how to manipulate, control, and coerce, I do not believe they always do so with ill intent. I don't think narcissists know any other way to interact with others. I know there is a good soul buried deep within each of them. I tried so hard to find the real person inside, but to no avail. In rare occurrences, I saw glimpses of their true selves.

Unfortunately, both Andrew and Jake preferred their fake selves over their true selves. It is very difficult to convince a narcissist that his true self is far more loveable and intriguing than his grandiose, inflated fake self. As hard as I tried, I finally had to accept the fact that I could not change them. Often we must accept the fact that the only person we can change is ourselves.

The Serenity Prayer

God, grant me the Serenity to accept
the things I cannot change,
Courage to change the things I can, and
Wisdom to know the difference.

I hope most of you who picked up this book thinking your loved one might be a narcissist found, in the end, he is not even close. For the rest of you who are now acknowledging the possibility, as I once did, that your loved one might be a pathological narcissist, you have a lot to sort out right now. I know the feeling is overwhelming. You have some big decisions to make.

The best advice I can give you right now is to be honest with yourself. Do not bury your head in the sand like I did for years. You have one chance at life. Make the most of it. Do the hard work now, so you do not spend the rest of your life unhappy and questioning yourself. Existing in such a state is no way for anyone to live. You deserve real, genuine love, and there are men out there who are capable of it.

I know this is much easier said than done, but I truly believe life has much to offer us if we simply choose to open our eyes to it and be honest with ourselves. We have the power to make changes in our lives, if we want. We must accept what we cannot change and change what we can.

In my situation, when it happened twice, I couldn't help but ask myself how I contributed to the problem. I would have to be asleep not to acknowledge the fact that there was a common thread in both of those relationships . . . me.

We learn from every experience in life. Some lessons are much harder than others. This one certainly wasn't easy, but I am truly grateful for what I learned from it. In both relationships I spent a long time refusing to acknowledge the truth. I denied the pain of my reality in order to avoid having to feel. Does this sound like anyone we know? Yes, this is exactly what I described a narcissist does when he disconnects from himself as a child. By doing this, you are able to avoid having to feel, right? You numb yourself from the pain.

Basically, by lying to yourself you are able to continue the relationship. Why would I want to lie to myself to continue such a relationship? Well, in the case of Andrew, I married him. The last thing any wife wants to acknowledge is that she is unhappy in her marriage. This is not something you easily accept, nor should it be. If you find you are unhappy, you should acknowledge it and work on things together to salvage your marriage.

What if you have done this, but nothing has improved and things have only grown worse? Well, in my case, you lie to yourself some more. Unfortunately, the more you lie to yourself, the more you disconnect from yourself.

Let's take a look at why I refused to acknowledge Jake's narcissistic tendencies? I had just gone through a divorce. Divorce is the failure of a committed relationship. Jake was the first serious boyfriend I'd had since my divorce. To fail at a second attempt at a committed relationship is extremely difficult to accept yourself, let alone to acknowledge openly to anyone.

So, what did I do? I lied to myself again. I did this subconsciously, of course. In order to live in the dark like this, one must disconnect from one's true self. You can't possibly be fully present and aware when in an unhappy relationship or situation. The more you lie to yourself, the more developed your false self becomes and the more you disconnect from your true self.

Remember, your true self is who you are when you feel most in touch with yourself. The false self is often used by individuals as a way to cover up their true feelings. The false self is inhibited and fearful. Once formed and functioning, the false self stifles the growth of the true self. The more developed one's false self becomes, the more nonexistent the true self becomes.[1]

I spent many years in this state, which I refer to as my "dark period." Eckhart Tolle refers to this state of being as the "pain-body." In his groundbreaking book, *The Power of Now*, he explains how the pain-body is actually afraid of the light of consciousness. Its survival is dependent on your unconscious fear of facing the pain that lives in you.[2]

In other words, you will remain in a state of pain, darkness, or unhappiness as long as you continue to lie to yourself and deny your reality. Resistance is what keeps us stuck in the unconscious realm. Tolle believes the more you resist the present moment, the more pain you create within yourself. The whole idea of Zen is to be so utterly and completely present in the now that no suffering can survive within you. Buddha defines enlightenment as the "end of suffering."[3]

In my opinion, the only true path to enlightenment is to drop all inner resistance and be honest. We must be true to ourselves. Certain events in my life forced me to face the truth about my marriage and my relationship with Jake. While both of these relationships ended badly, the second time around I discovered a therapy that helped me find myself again.

Psychotherapy is probably the most well-known or commonly sought type of therapy. The basis of psychotherapy, or talk therapy, is to ask patients to reflect on their past to potentially find some deep root cause for their pain. I did this for years and it never helped me, for I was blessed with a very happy childhood and wonderful parents.

Cognitive Behavioral Therapy (CBT) is a type of treatment that has been around for the last forty to fifty years, but has just recently been gaining popularity. This type of therapy is based on the belief that emotional disturbance is caused by distorted or irrational reasoning. It suggests that humans have a tendency to think illogically. This warped way of thinking can be acquired at any point in a person's life.[4]

Cognitive therapy teaches us that others do not upset us, we upset and disturb ourselves as a result of the negative views we take of things. Much disturbance comes from the belief that we should be able to control others in an attempt to control ourselves. Unfortunately, what we fail to realize is that the only person we can control is ourselves.

Tolle explains that we all have a voice in our head that reminds us of troubles from our past and encourages us to worry about our future. Some individuals listen to this voice more than others. Certain events or experiences can cause this voice in our head to run incessantly.

Tolle believes all negativity is caused by too much focus on the past or future. He explains that worry and anxiety are caused by too much future focus and not enough presence. Being stuck in the past, either feeling resentful or guilty, is a result of too much past and not enough presence. By focusing on the past or future and denying the reality of your present, you remain stuck in the pain-body. Identification with your mind causes thought to be compulsive. This mental noise prevents you from finding the realm of inner stillness inside you that is necessary to achieve enlightenment.[5]

Cognitive Behavioral Therapy is a "doing" therapy whereby the therapist takes you through different mental exercises in an effort to help retrain your brain. We easily get stuck in negative patterns of thinking. However, the good news is we can retrain our brain though behavioral therapy.[6]

This therapy is not easy. The exercises can be difficult and at times provoke anxiety. However, with the assistance of a trained Cognitive Behavioral Therapist, it is extremely effective and worth every bit of hard work.

I'm sure you have heard the expression, "What doesn't kill us only makes us stronger." Well, this has certainly been the case for me. I finally surrendered. What did I surrender? My ego. I stopped lying to myself that everything was okay. I dropped all inner resistance and started being honest with myself.

I have learned and strongly believe that it is not what happens to you that matters in life, but how you respond to it that determines your overall happiness and success. I feel a sense of inner peace now that I never knew was possible. I am certain I would not have gotten to this point so early in my life had I not experienced what I did.

I know I have only touched the surface of enlightenment and have much more to learn, but it feels wonderful and I want you to know: true happiness is possible. First, you must determine if you are in a relationship with a narcissist. Once you are honest with yourself about the reality of your situation and the part you are playing in it, you are on the path to true consciousness and awakening.

We all make mistakes. It's okay to make mistakes. It's part of being human. As humans, we have the ability to admit when we are wrong and learn from our mistakes. Behind every mistake lies the potential to grow and evolve. Evolution is a beautiful thing.

We should never be afraid to ask for support from others in our quest to evolve. I believe we are all interconnected. If we need to heal, we must reach out to others. If you have learned anything from my story, I hope you have learned that people only hurt themselves when they disconnect or withdraw from others. Being afraid to ask for help only leads to further isolation. Humans cannot thrive in isolation.

Do not endure this alone. Reach out to a family member, friend, or mental health professional. If you don't feel there is anyone you can talk to about your situation and are looking for additional support, please visit my website and message board at www.lisaescott.com.

Whatever you decide, I encourage you to always live your life consciously and with full awareness. I know it will not always be easy, but I can tell you from my experience, it will feel "right." This feeling of "rightness" has brought me a sense of serenity I never knew was possible. I want you to experience this same feeling, and it is my hope that you will stay true to yourself and your feelings, and by doing this you will find the clarity you need to live your life to its fullest. You deserve it.

Notes

1. Charles Whitfield, *Healing the Child Within* (Deerfield Beach, FL: Health Communications, 1987).
2. Eckhart Tolle, *The Power of Now* (Vancouver, BC: Namestate Publishing, 1999), 38.
3. Ibid.

4. Fred Penzel, *Obsessive-Compulsive Disorders* (New York: Oxford University Press, 2000).

5. Tolle, *The Power of Now.*

6. Penzel, *Obsessive-Compulsive Disorders.*

Book Club Questions

1. Can a narcissist ever be cured?

2. Are relationships possible with a narcissist?

3. Why does a narcissist want to be in a committed relationship?

4. How can you recognize a narcissist before it's too late?

5. Why do some women stay in relationships with narcissists?

6. Does our society celebrate and reward narcissistic behavior?

7. Does a narcissist really love himself as much as he portrays?

8. What kind of parent does a narcissist make?

9. Will a narcissist ever truly be happy?

About the Author

Lisa E. Scott is a native of the Chicagoland area. She lives and works downtown as a human resources professional. She has been published twice in academic journals related to her profession. This is her first work of a personal nature. In addition to writing, Lisa enjoys playing the piano and singing. Visit her at www.lisaescott.com.

0 26575 52187 0